The Collaborative Playwright

D1566329

The Collaborative Playwright

Practical Advice for Getting Your Play Written

Bruce Graham
and
Michele Volansky

HEINEMANN
Portsmouth, NH

Heinemann
A division of Reed Elsevier Inc.
361 Hanover Street
Portsmouth, NH 03801–3912
www.heinemanndrama.com

Offices and agents throughout the world

The authors and publisher wish to thank those who have generously given permission
to reprint borrowed material:

Excerpts from *Coyote on a Fence* by Bruce Graham. Copyright © 2000 by Bruce Graham.
Published by Dramatists Play Service, Inc.

Excerpts from *Burkie* by Bruce Graham. Copyright © 1989 by Bruce Graham. Published
by Dramatists Play Service, Inc.

Excerpts from *The Champagne Charlie Stakes* by Bruce Graham. Copyright © 1993 by
Bruce Graham. Published by Dramatists Play Service, Inc.

Excerpts from *Belmont Avenue Social Club* by Bruce Graham. Copyright © 1993 by Bruce
Graham. Published by Dramatists Play Service, Inc.

CAUTION: The scenes from *Coyote on a Fence*, *Burkie*, *The Champagne Charlie Stakes*, and
Belmont Avenue Social Club included in this volume are reprinted by permission of the
author. The English language stock and amateur stage performance rights in these Plays
are controlled exclusively by Dramatists Play Service, Inc., 440 Park Avenue South, New
York, NY 10016. No professional or nonprofessional performance of the Plays may be
given without obtaining, in advance, the written permission of Dramatists Play Service,
Inc., and paying the requisite fee. Inquiries concerning all other rights should be
addressed to Harden-Curtis Associates, 850 Seventh Avenue, Suite 903, New York, NY
10019. Attn: Mary Harden.

Graham, Bruce, 1957–
    The collaborative playwright : practical advice for getting your play written / Bruce
Graham and Michele Volansky.
        p. cm.
    ISBN-13: 978-0-325-00995-7
    ISBN-10: 0-325-00995-3
    1. Playwriting.   I. Volansky, Michele.   II. Title.

PN1661.G67 2007
808.2—dc22   2007000624

Editors: Lisa A. Barnett and Danny Miller
Production service: Lisa S. Garboski, *bookworks*
Production coordination: Vicki Kasabian
Cover design: Joni Doherty Design
Typesetter: Valerie Levy / Drawing Board Studios
Manufacturing: Jamie Carter

Printed in the United States of America on acid-free paper
11   10   09   08   07   VP   1   2   3   4   5

Dedicated to our students—
past, present, and future

CONTENTS

Caroline Luft ◘ Kris Elgstrand ◘ Laura Eason ◘ Dennis Reardon ◘ Rinne Groff ◘
Jeffrey Hatcher ◘ J. T. Rogers ◘ Lisa Dillman ◘ Gina Gionfriddo ◘ Nick Wardigo
◘ Tracy Letts ◘ Austin Pendleton ◘ Christopher Shinn ◘ Tom Donaghy ◘ Jose
Rivera ◘ Tracey Scott Wilson ◘ Jon Klein ◘ Melanie Marnich ◘ Larry Loebell ◘
Evan Smith ◘ Kimberly Senior Baker ◘ Lisa McNulty ◘ Pam MacKinnon ◘ Aaron
Posner ◘ Russ Tutterow ◘ Les Waters ◘ Jessica Thebus ◘ Lon Winston ◘
Cynthia Croot ◘ Paul Meshejian ◘ Lee Devin ◘ Sara Garonzik ◘ Mary Harden

PREFACE

WHY I BECAME A PLAYWRIGHT

My old man was a plumber and when I was little he'd occasionally take me on a job with him. At the age of five I spent a memorable winter day with him in a block of apartments under construction, which contained a room full of empty appliance boxes. For a kid with an imagination, row after row of Westinghouse refrigerator cartons was better than Disneyland. (Hey, we were poor.) The old man even gave me a sharp object to cut out windows and doors. (Today this might be seen as unwise. Ahh, the sixties were a great time.) As late afternoon approached, however, I began to freeze and went looking for dad.

I found him squeezed into a crawl space lying on a piece of cardboard, trying in vain to ward off the effects of the cold concrete floor. His hands, filthy from wrestling with pipes all day, were cracked and bleeding. The only warmth he'd had all day came from his small acetylene torch.

As we walked to the car—him lugging a toolbox that weighed more than me—I realized something important: I never wanted a job like this.

I didn't want cracked, bloody hands. I wanted to be warm and not carry anything heavier than a briefcase. I wanted to get up when I felt like it and work till I felt like quitting. I wanted to go to parties, meet lots of girls, and make a ton of money.

So I became a playwright.

And—except for that ton of money thing—the rest all came true.

I can't write prose. Bores the hell out of me. Describing a room, a sunset, a woman's smile, is torture. You need an eye to write a novel, which I don't have. (My wife once proved this theory by asking me the color of our bed-room. I got it on the third guess.)

A playwright writes with his/her ear. You can be as visual as you want—write reams describing your set, costumes, even—as in the case of O'Neill—your characters. But it's all pretty much a waste of time since the budget probably won't allow everything you want, your director and designers have their thoughts, and the actor you can't live without just isn't as tall as you have written in the script.

Who cares about the color of the wallpaper? That's for when you're in preproduction. When you sit facing the empty notebook, it's what the charac-ters say and do that's important. Worry about that other stuff later. It's tough enough putting interesting characters into a fascinating plot without getting bogged down in the style of someone's shoes.

During this book I'll be making lots of references to my own work. I do this for a few reasons:

1. I don't have to get permission for the rights.
2. You might become intrigued enough to buy copies, which cranks up my royalties. (They make great gifts, by the way.)
3. I can describe in detail how these plays came to be. (Not to mention filling up pages with lots of amusing anecdotes.) I can't honestly say where other playwrights get their inspiration, but I can pretty much explain where I got mine.

Okay, let's get something out in the open right now. I am totally untrained as a playwright. Never went to Yale. Hell, I barely got out of Indiana University of Pennsylvania.

My training was as an actor. When I went to New York right out of college I found there wasn't a huge market for short, balding young character actors. So I decided to start writing plays with parts for short, balding young charac-ter actors. And they always ended up casting a tall guy with hair.

I didn't just decide overnight to become a playwright. I'd written plays and comedy sketches in high school. I spent three years making money as a stand-up comic and creating material. But training? I finally had a playwriting course in grad school at Villanova. By that time I'd had two plays off-Broad-way and was published. I skipped the class a lot. I got a B.

I learned to write plays by watching them, reading them, and being in them. I was in my thirties when I finally discovered that a guy named Aristotle laid down some very practical rules for writing plays. Wish I'd known this earlier. Would've saved me some trouble.

Since I'll be making some references to *The Poetics* I thought it might be good to bring it up now. Sure, it's a bit dry. And some of the advice is a bit dated. ("A character should be good. Even a woman or a slave can be good.") But at its core, there's some good stuff in there.

Aristotle lists what a good play needs. It needs a character with a strong "want." It needs conflict. It needs spectacle, which means "something to look at." It needs a character who changes during the course of the story.

And it needs a "thought" behind it. More on this later.

So, once you're done with this book, go and check out Aristotle. (Feel free to skip over the really boring parts.)

WHY I BECAME A DRAMATURG

My family tells stories. We live for it. We also like to listen to stories. However, our dinner table is one of the toughest rooms one will ever play—if your stories are not good, we will take you down.

I learned fairly early on that while I did have some gifts in the storytelling department, I was a much better responder; that is, I was the one who would, in fact, take a bad storyteller down. There was mocking, there was cajoling, there was shame.

All of which leads to superb dramaturgy.

I'm joking, of course. Sort of. Good dramaturgs are those special individuals who can listen acutely, respond appropriately, and, with equal parts tact and tenacity, can assess the success and failure of a given work, all the while offering helpful options of how to proceed. I don't want to rewrite a playwright's play. I want them to write the play that they are yearning to write.

One of the most exciting things about being a dramaturg (okay, so it isn't all that exciting a career—we take our joys where we can) is working with a playwright over a long period of time, on a number of different plays, and from a variety of starting positions.

While I do not have the actual playwriting experience that my esteemed colleague has, I have been around hundreds of writers at all levels—from the emerging to the award-winning (not sure where my colleague fits in here . . .) and I've taught playwriting for years. I know a thing or two about what doesn't work, and a couple more things about what does.

I had the benefit, in writing this book, of having an extraordinary collaborator. Because Bruce and I have worked together before, we had a common vocabulary and a shorthand that became enormously helpful. We also have very little ego when it comes to "ownership." You'll notice throughout the book that we have inserted "interjections" and "other opinions," as well as used the word "I." The "I" in this case is actually a happy merger between Volansky and Graham. It is an example of collaboration in action. I hope every playwright can have such a colleague.

A word about that teaching playwriting thing. I'm not one hundred percent convinced that writing can be taught. Bruce and I will give you a great deal of suggestions, helpful hints, and insights into what makes a good play. But at the end of the day, you still have to do it. You and you alone have to have your own passion, your own drive, and your own point of view.

Good luck.

1
CHAPTER

Generating Ideas

AS A KID ONE OF MY BIGGEST THRILLS WAS EAVESDROPPING ON ADULTS. (I told you we were poor.) On the rare occasions my parents would entertain I would sit at the top of the stairs in my pajamas listening. When their voices would get really low, I strained to hear because that was the stuff they didn't want the kids to hear.

This was great training for a young playwright, since dialogue and character interaction are the essence of playwriting. Sure, plot and structure are important, but when you break it down to the most basic component, plays are people talking to each other. (Or, in the case of Terrence McNally, people talking to each other about opera.)

A playwright deals with human behavior (or misbehavior) and therefore must become a student of human beings. You can study all the great plays, memorize Aristotelian rules for drama, subscribe to the Sunday *Times*, and attend play readings till you can't face another plastic cup full of cheap red wine again, but if you don't understand what makes other people tick, then you are certainly not cut out to be a playwright. "Hey, easy," you say. "I see people all the time." Yeah, well, I see football games all the time but that doesn't mean I can run out there and do it.

Observing people is something that's not easy for one primary reason: You have to sit on your own ego. Our first inclination in any social interaction is to usually focus on us. As a playwright your focus has to be fully on your subject. Don't bother telling all your stories—you already know them. What is this person's background? How does it shape his/her worldview? So, that's rule number one: study people.

One of the biggest myths in any form of writing—and the one that stops a lot of writers before they even get started—is that in order to be inspired a thunderbolt must strike you in the head, causing a lightbulb to go off, which in turn makes said writer leap up shouting, "Eureka!" while grabbing wildly for a pen.

Yeah, I wish.

How many times have you heard—or said—something to the effect of, "My life would make a great play." (Or "movie" or "novel." Fill in the blank.)

The weird thing is, almost everyone's life would make a good play. The difference between a playwright and some-loudmouth-spouting-this-theory-in-a-bar is that the playwright knows how to do it.

Your life is filled with conflict, tension, joy, tragedy, action, unanswered questions, anger, sex, comedy, music. All the things you need for a play. The question becomes about how you pick and choose what part of your life you want to write about. (Of course, you could always become a "performance artist" and tell us everything. This should also include lengthy speculation on your body parts. See Chapter 13 in our next book—"How to Get a Good Review in the *New York Times*.")

SUGGESTION ONE: USE YOUR FAMILY

Almost all of us either start with or eventually use our families for material. Williams with *Glass Menagerie*, Hellman with *Little Foxes*, O'Neill with *Long Day's Journey into Night*, Simon with the Double-B trilogy (*Brighton Beach, Biloxi Blues, Broadway Bound*), Anderson with *I Never Sang for My Father*—the list goes on.

These plays differ wildly in theme, style—even time period. But the one thing these plays have in common is that the authors have chosen a specific incident within the family to dramatize: finding a suitor for sister in *Menagerie* or a business deal in *Foxes*.

All these plays take an isolated incident to drive the play, and then fill it with characters that are quirky and interesting and real, because they come straight from the author's memory. This is a very easy way of creating characterization and for the most part, it works. Why rack your brain coming up with an interesting character when you've got a whole dinner table full of them?

Burkie, my first professionally produced play, is a good example of the use-your-family genre. Briefly, it's about a brother and sister dealing with their dying father. It's not a brilliantly original story line by any measure. And I had no interest in writing about cancer or euthanasia, both of which have been used by marketing people to describe the play. (Boy, that sells tickets: "Let's go see that cancer play.")

To me *Burkie* was always about a generation of men, World War II vets, who were taught at a very early age to repress emotions. This was something I observed not only in my own family, but also among others in my neighborhood, too. None of my buddies' dads were able to show any emotion either. When my mother, a former schoolteacher, had a battle with breast cancer I saw my father struggling to deal with all the emotional crap that occurs when someone you love is in pain. This is what propelled the play.

Okay, now I've got the characters and what Aristotle calls the "thought" of the play. In other words, I know what I want to say and the people I want to say it. Now comes the tough part: How are they going to say it in a way that keeps the audience interested for two hours? I find my family fascinating but that's because they're my family. How can I make them fascinating to your family? There's the rub.

So I chose one incident: the arrival of the sister, an ex-jock with a successful chain of sporting goods stores, with "news" (she's pregnant) and used that as a catalyst for the play. The son was a classical pianist, sacrificing his career to take care of dad, causing resentment towards sister. Then, to keep the tension rising, I made it all take place in one night. (Volansky says that this is something a lot of the above family plays have in common: a tight time frame. We like to call it an "internal clock.")

There's a fine line to using your family, however. Just how much do you want to be true, and how much of the truth must you distort in order to have an interesting story?

Let's look at what's "true" in *Burkie*:

1. Yes, my father was a plumber. (That's in case you missed the introduction.)
2. I have an older sister who was an athlete and moved away from the neighborhood. She also threw all her sports trophies in the garbage. (You can't make this stuff up.)
3. My mother was a schoolteacher who died of cancer.
4. My father was a WW II vet stationed in the Philippines.
5. My parents both had fathers with drinking problems.

Notice, all of the above have to do with characterization.

Now, here's the stuff that isn't true:

1. My father did not die of cancer. (As of this writing he's 79, in good health, and cutting my lawn.)
2. My sister never had to keep her pregnancy a secret. On the contrary, I think my parents took out ads in the paper.
3. My sister is not a wealthy, driven businesswoman. (She's a school-teacher. We all know how much money they make.)
4. There is no tension or unspoken, unpleasant history between my sister and me. At least I don't think so. (We actually get along pretty well and did as kids, too.)
5. I do not play the piano. (Never have, doubt at this point I ever will.)

Now notice, almost all the above deal with plot. If my father is still alive and doing my landscaping, I have no story. If I used real life in the brother/sister relationship it would be extremely dull. People who get along do not make for interesting drama.

So, use your family, but be open to changing the stuff that doesn't work. And 99 percent of the time, the changes you make are for plot purposes.

SUGGESTION TWO: "I WANNA CHANGE THE WORLD"

Okay, now you've used up your family, and holiday dinners are especially tense because mom thought you used too much profanity and dad didn't like the fact that the actor who played him was fat. What do you do now? Where does that next play come from? Your own ego, of course.

If you want to write a play, you damn well better have something interesting to say. There's nothing worse than a writer without a point of view. So sit back, think about what really pisses you off in life (if you're like me that should take about nine seconds) and decide, through your skill as a playwright, to solve the problem.

Example: I'm a senior at Indiana University of Pennsylvania taking World Religions for one of my humanities credits. To my surprise, the class is fascinating.

However, I'm the only senior amongst a bunch of freshmen. Freshmen from western Pennsylvania. The kind of kids raised in towns where the leading industry is "live bait" and people greet each other by saying "Get'cher deer?"

Me? I'm the slick big-city kid from the east—a true snob to these bumpkins—and get a real kick as the professor makes them squirm uncomfortably by challenging some of their beliefs. He'll describe one of the traits of Buddhists, perhaps, and after the rabble openly scoff at it, he'll turn it around and show a similar trait among Christians.

So I'm sitting in the back of the class—I always sit in the back—and I'm really beginning to dislike these other students. Short of tossing grenades, how can I straighten them out?

Okay, so now I've got my "cause." I want to show these clowns the folly of their intolerance. The irony that my own intolerance towards them drove this story does not come to me until years later.

How do I make all this into a play? This epiphany came to me, literally, in that class in the form of a fantasy: Boy, I'd love to sit down and have a couple beers with God. This is what I scribbled down in my notebook.

Ask yourself, how many times a day do you say things like that? Probably more than you realize. And you wouldn't be alone:

"Boy, that 'American Dream' thing really corrupts people." (Miller)

"Hmmm . . . how would two disenfranchised bums deal with the apocalypse?" (Beckett)

"Hey, I know a lot about opera. Maybe I should write about it. Over and over . . ." (McNally)

"Wouldn't it be cool if black people didn't show up one day and white people had to fend for themselves?" (Ward)

"I wonder what it's like to bang a goat?" (Albee)

Now, I wasn't there so I can't say this is how these plays originated, but you get the idea. We ask ourselves rhetorical questions countless times a day. If these things are on our minds, maybe they're on someone else's, too. Someone crazy enough to buy a ticket.

Okay, now I've got my "cause" (straighten out the young rednecks) and my rhetorical question (beer/God). Good start, but I still need a story.

Enter fantasy. And this is a very important part of playwriting. It's your world! The second the houselights dim you are in charge. So, what fascinates you?

I've always had a morbid interest in the apocalypse. *On the Beach*, *Dr. Strangelove*, *Fail Safe Devil* were all movies that fascinated me as a kid. Being born at the tail end of the Eisenhower years, I still remember air raid drills, wherein we first graders would climb under our desks in case of nuclear attack. The fact that our desks were not lead lined with provisions for two hundred years never entered into the picture.

However, huddling under a desk waiting for the big one to drop can leave an impression on a six-year-old.

Now, this sounds crazy and you're probably wondering what the hell this has to do with playwriting. Is this guy going to go off on tangents through the whole book?

The point is this: you have to bring your entire life to a play. Things that made an impact—good or bad—as a child have been buried up there for a long time. (The bad stuff usually makes for better drama, but the good things can be used for comedy relief.) Sometimes I have no idea where thoughts, dialogue, or characters come from. I'm not big on introspection when I'm in the middle of a script because it tends to slow me down. But if your instincts take you in a direction, go with it. Don't question where it came from, write it down! There's time to think about where it came from later.

For instance, in *Coyote on a Fence*, the character Bobby has a monologue about his first bike. Now, I like to think I have very little in common with Bobby, a racist skinhead mass murderer, but the story of his first bike is the story of my first bike. And it wasn't till weeks later, when I was typing it up, that I realized it. Had I stopped to question it ("Gee, do I really want to share my memories with this guy?") I might not have written it. Sometimes thinking too much when writing a play is a dangerous thing.

SUGGESTION THREE: GET UP AND LOOK AROUND

Unless you're one of those writers with a great imagination eventually you're going to run out of ideas. Now it's time to go out and look for a story. Believe it or not, they're out there. Sometimes they're delivered right to your door.

An Associated Press article in the *Philadelphia Inquirer* grabbed my attention one morning. It dealt with a death row inmate in Texas named James Beathard who published a newsletter, *The Texas Death Row Journal*.

Okay, nothing so far, until the third paragraph, where he speaks about writing obituaries for fellow inmates. Now the playwriting senses kick in. Writing obituaries for men who actually know the date and time of their deaths. Men who can collaborate on their own death notice. This is something I can honestly say I've never seen on stage.

Then it got better. One of the hardest things James had to do in some cases was to come up with something positive to say about the other inmates. No matter how much compassion James had (and it was a lot, believe me) some of these guys were impossible to find anything nice to write about in a sentence, let alone an entire obituary.

Bang! Character, conflict, setting, even Aristotle's "thought"; is there a kernel of good in all men, even those we consider (often rightly so) monsters? I knew I had a play, all from one newspaper article.

I keep a folder full of yellowed news articles that I show my students. Possible story ideas. The article on James is in there along with a few others I've used.

One story gave me a great character: an autograph hound. This was a guy I'd actually met (he'd asked for my autograph; he'd even hang around outside the stage door for "Disney on Ice") and when I saw the article I had to put it in the file.

First of all, it was a character that came with an instant "want." He's constantly in pursuit of the celebrity, no matter how minor, to scribble in his little book. What made this guy especially memorable was the fact that he had a whole science to this thing; he'd carry a suitcase with changes of clothes so that he might disguise himself and get two autographs. And—this was the best part—in the article it showed him mentoring a young guy in the art. Now I had two wants and a reason for him to be talking about his craft.

But I never did anything with it. Then I got a call from a local PBS station looking for monologues. Went to the folder, found my autograph hound, and found my monologue.

One more out of the pile: A city block in a quiet uproar because a neighbor—an elderly woman—feeds the pigeons every day and their stoops are covered with pigeon crap. Why would this story make the file?

Easy. For all its simplicity, this could be a complicated little story. The neighbors have a legitimate beef, but the old lady, housebound by illness, found that her only joy came from feeding those pigeons. To a playwright, this is what should catch your attention. A clear-cut conflict peopled with characters who are trying to do the right thing, but still want to put an end to the problem. If the old lady was a mean old bitch there's no complication: call the cops, shoot the pigeons, burn her house down, all sorts of resolutions. But the fact that she was a sympathetic character doing something unsympathetic made her story—at least to me—rather interesting. This one also got pulled out of the file when PBS called again, now looking for a half-hour story.

So three stories—all produced in one form or another—and taken right from the newspaper.

In order to do this you have to develop your dramatist instincts. The paper's full of conflicts, but which ones have human beings we care about in situations that keep our interest?

That's your job.

A DRAMATURGICAL INTERJECTION

I would also make a case for the fact that if you need to generate ideas, then the play isn't being driven out of some *deep need*. I personally love plays that fully embrace and reveal a playwright's deep need. I can spot one a mile away: *Angels in America* is one. A *Streetcar Named Desire* is another. I would argue that *Burkie* is a fantastic example of one.

However, as we have observed, the muse doesn't always make her entrance on cue, and so we need to do some digging around in your psyche to dredge up something that might be of use.

Many great plays are generated from the playwright's personal story, or stories, in the case of Bruce Graham (he's got a million of them). While I have read my share of "it's a major holiday, the family is all gathered at the cabin, I suppose now is the time to come out of the closet" plays, I still believe that the things that have happened to you, or the things that get under your skin, or in your heart, are the things that make the best plays.

One of my favorite ways of tapping into these personal stories comes from an exercise I call "Memory Writing." It's a fairly standard exercise, but it is one you can use again and again, because every time you do it, your mind takes you to a different place.

MEMORY WRITING EXERCISE 1

On the top of a blank piece of paper, write out your full name. Look at it for a while. Think about who this person is, has been, or could be.

Now list all the nicknames that this person has had. Be honest. If you were called "Ratface" on the schoolyard, please include it. What are the various contexts for these nicknames? What are the feelings, memories that are associated with each? Who are the people connected with a given nickname?

Next, write out the birth date of this person. What are other events that happened on this day? For example, I was born in Camden two days after

Martin Luther King was assassinated—making me considerably younger than Bruce Graham—and the entire city was on fire. Have any of these other events intersected with your life? If not, why? If so, in what ways?

List at least eight events in this life. They don't have to be revelatory, like coming out to your entire family in a cabin on a major American holiday, just things you can recall. They can be moments, or full-blown memories. On my list, I often put the day I dumped my little sister out of her red wagon onto the sidewalk in front of my parents' house. Sometimes I include a game I used to play as a child, "airline stewardess" (don't ask). The possibilities are endless. Take a close look at the quality and type of the events you have listed.

Select one of the events and start writing, *in medias res*. You all know that phrase, "in the middle of things." Don't give us backstory, don't describe, just get in there. Who are the characters involved? What are the things you remember them saying? What do you *wish* they had said, done, or felt? Allow your brain to take you away from the "reality" and into the world of "possibility."

Lather, rinse, repeat seven more times.

A DRAMATURGICAL INTERJECTION

My family was about as poor as Graham's. My dad taught at a Catholic high school and the "entertainment" funds were generally in short supply. However, we always had a grand time on Sunday afternoons. We would pile into the wagon and head from South Jersey to the Philadelphia International Airport.

For about four hours every Sunday, I would sit with my dad and my siblings and watch planes take off and land. As we were sitting there, my dad would point out this person or that person, saying this or doing that. We would listen attentively, sometimes stare and then discuss.

What does this little walk down memory lane mean to you? It means go to the airport. Go to the bus station. Go to the train station. People who are coming and going *always* have a story to tell. They are usually full of the emotions that are the basis of a good play: anxiety, hope, sadness, joy, panicked, restrained, discouraged. They also talk talk talk, most often in ways that inform us of who they are as people. Some people swear more, some people pretend to be someone they are not (true story: I once told a woman on an airplane that I was traveling to take the deposition of a serial bad check writer). These public places are all great spots to people watch, and generate characters and circumstances. Here's another exercise to use.

MEMORY WRITING EXERCISE 2

Make a list (have I mentioned that I think lists are the basis of all writing?) of all the people that you encounter daily, someone you might see at the bus stop, at lunch, getting your coffee. What have you imagined their habits to be? Who are the members of their family? What are their hopes, anxieties? What do you imagine they do when you are not around? What might you have in common with them? How are you different?

Select two of these characters and put them in a room with each other. The opening line, said by either, is "There's a bee in your bonnet." Write no fewer than twenty lines of dialogue for each character.

Why is this a good exercise for generating ideas? For me, it puts two seemingly unrelated people in contact with one another, creating an immediate sense of tension. People, for the most part, need a bit of time to become *completely* comfortable around another human. They don't relax until they are sure where they stand.

The other thing this exercise does is that it takes a random phrase and activates it. What does it mean, really, to each of these characters? How do they respond to it? Is it funny or maudlin? Is it a threat or an observation?

You can also try other common phrases. "Pass the salt," "Nice weather we're having," and "Is someone sitting here" have all been used to generate plays that are driven by characters. We'll talk about building characters in another chapter.

I would also make a case for looking at your personal belief systems as a way to come up with an idea for a play.

A digression: I should say that I am not advocating the "political/social themed" play. Chances are high that if you set out to write your opus on "abortion" or "gun control" or "my allowance," you are going to write a bad play.

What I am advocating is the personalization of major political or social themes. There are actual, live human beings on each side of any issue and these people make for great characters in a play.

I owe a special thanks to dramaturg Michael Bigelow Dixon for the following exercise, on which I have riffed a little.

EXERCISE

First, make a list of five issues of which you understand both sides; that is, you can imagine what kinds of conversations take place around each issue. What are the "nonnegotiables" for each side? Is there a hierarchy for each of these? What are the known things, and what are the unknown things?

Now list five pairs of people. These can be "known" people, like George and Martha or Lewis and Clark (hell, it could be Lewis and Martin), or it could be unknown, generic people, like a mother and daughter, a teacher and student, a playwright and dramaturg.

Next list five public locations. I say public because people behave differently when they are in public. After you do this exercise once, you can then do it again and put the people in a private place. This public place could be an airport, a restaurant, a hotel lobby.

Using only one pair of the characters (no waiters, nurses, or aliens are allowed to be added), place them in one of the public settings and have them discuss one of the issues.

What is the usefulness of this exercise?

It gives you, the playwright, the opportunity to investigate how you feel about issues beyond yourself. It allows you to explore people who must come to some peace or finality with another character. Finally, it encourages you to pull back the lens (a phrase I *love* to use) and think about the *context* in which you are writing.

One thing we have not talked about is the diligence required to be a playwright. And when I think about diligence, I think of Bruce. He writes *every day*, regardless of what it is. When he is blocked, I suspect he just starts riffing and uses some of these "generating ideas" exercises. Sometimes they bear fruit, sometimes they don't. But what he does is practice the craft of writing—putting pen to paper, or fingers to keypad. As I mentioned before, you cannot wait for the muse to strike you, so make a habit of carving out time *every day* to write something.

2

CHAPTER

Prewriting and Outlines

ABOUT THE DUMBEST THING A WRITER CAN DO IS GET UP IN THE MORN-ing, state to the world, "I'm going to write my play," and then sit down at the computer and start.

Unless, of course, you've warmed up.

I was perhaps the worst cross country runner in the history of Ridley High School, but I did learn one thing: You never start any sort of marathon without doing some serious stretching. The same is true for writing a play.

We've already looked at some of the sources for story and characters. You've found this advice incredibly useful and now you're ready to roll. You are ready to write the next great American theatrical masterpiece.

Wrong. Start your warmup.

THE OUTLINE

I like to compare a play outline to starting on a trip. You have to make sure there's a destination—at least a vague one. You can say you're going to California, but it might be San Diego, might be San Francisco.

In other words, you should have a general idea how the play is going to end. If it's a love story, you shouldn't start before you know whether or not the couple will be together at the final curtain. If it is a thriller, you should know who did it. If it is psychological realism, you should know who needs to see the shrink. You don't have to have the final moment—or even the final line of dialogue—but you have to know what emotion you want the audience to be feeling when the houselights come back on.

So don't get bogged down by saying, "Oh, my God, I can't start this play. I have no idea what the final moment will be." Have a vague direction (California) but worry about the city later.

An Example of the Above as a Digression: This, by the way, does not mean you can't change your destination during the rewrite process. The original final moment of *Burkie* had Jon sitting in a bar saying, "I don't feel like goin' home right now."

During rehearsals we realized that was no resolution at all. If Jon had said that, he would have gone through the whole play and never changed, which, for those keeping score is really bad for a character. Besides, it took a downer play and threw an even more downer last line into the mix.

The last line just didn't work and I was going nuts trying to fix it. Finally, I went back and looked at the opening moments and found it: "I never said there was." Now, this makes no sense out of context, but it basically signaled a final understanding—a reconciliation if you will—between father and son. It allowed a small change for Jon's character and a very, very slight feeling of optimism at the end of the play. I was close in the first draft, but still a few miles off my final destination. (Or as Bugs Bunny would say, "I shoulda' made a left turn at Al-ba-quoik-ie.")

And, for the record, I later used "I don't feel like goin' home right now," as the final line in *Coyote on a Fence*. If it doesn't work in one play, save it for another. This is called recycling.

BACK TO THE OUTLINE

An outline can be as formal or informal as you like. If you're particularly anal you might prefer the classic Roman numeral outline. Knock yourself out. Me? I prefer the write-a-lot-of-ideas-down-and-draw-arrows outline.

Although I may cut some slack on the final moment of the play, there is one rule that is absolute: *You do not start a two-act play until you know what the end of the first act will be!*

Why? Because the end of the first act is what will drive your second act.

A DRAMATURGICAL INTERJECTION

Of all the lessons one might learn in this book, what Bruce just spelled out in regard to the end of the first act is perhaps the most significant because of all the implications it generates.

One of the most frustrating things I've encountered when reading new work is what I call the "second act slump." Playwrights can be brilliant at tossing balls into the air (exciting, colorful, and profoundly witty balls) and then, for a certain period of time, keeping them afloat in ways that make an audience gasp and applaud. However, nine times out of ten, the second act starts and the balls start smashing to the ground. The playwright has made smart decisions about the kinds of characters and actions they want to investigate, but has not fully thought through the conflict or the resolution.

When you know what the trajectory of the play is, you can backtrack and figure out how your characters need to act or respond in order to have an *internal logic.*

Let me elaborate. When you are working on your outline and doing the prewriting work that we will cover below, it is imperative that you have some sense (and I'm talking even the vaguest of notions) about what the conflict is, how it might be resolved, and who is going to be participating in it. It drives me bonkers when I feel like I have to demand a play to *get to the point.*

BACK TO BRUCE

Another digression: I'm a sophomore in college and have just written a hilarious first act of a play based on the house where I live. Great characters, sparkling one-liners. I give it to my high school drama teacher to read, and she hands it back like a dead fish saying, "I left at intermission. Something has to happen in the first act to make me come back and see the second." That quote should be hanging above every playwright's desk.

The audience needs that moment when they say, "Wow, I wonder what happens next." I don't even go out and buy the new notebook until I have that moment.

The unanswered question is a great way to end the act, or in some cases, to drive the entire play. (David Mamet says that every play has a question that must be answered. We love that.) In Peter Schaffer's *Equus* we find out in the first ten minutes that a boy blinded six horses. I don't know about you, but my curiosity was piqued. Why did he do it? By the end of the play, he tells us.

On a smaller scale, good use of the unanswered question is Albee's *The Zoo Story.* In the first moments Jerry announces, "I've been to the zoo. You'll read about it in the papers tomorrow, or maybe see it in television."

Sitting out there in the audience I start percolating: Who is this guy? What happened at the zoo? Why would it be in the papers?

And, being a smart playwright, Mr. Albee holds off on telling us till the final moments.

So, the most common way to engage your audience—and bring them back for the second act—is to introduce new information right before intermission. Information that provokes an unanswered question.

Here's how I've done it in *Burkie*—Jon informs Jess that Ed wants to kill himself and that she should keep her pregnancy a secret. "Just give me tonight. Watch him, listen to him, and in the morning—if you still want to give him 'Something to live for' you go and tell him you're pregnant. But not tonight."

Now the audience has some unanswered questions: What happens to Ed at night? Will Jess keep the bargain? What happens if she does tell him?

Are you on the edge of your seat? No, it's not that kind of play. But for a family drama, that's enough.

In a more plot-oriented show you need something a little more dramatic. *Minor Demons* is a pretty plot-heavy play. Lawyer returns to his hometown and defends a psychotic kid on a murder charge. Then lawyer finds out his best friend, a cop, screwed everything up and the kid could walk. What's important is that the lawyer discovers this the same time that the audience does.

Now the audience—who always wants to be one step ahead of you—starts pondering: Will he get the kid off? Will he cover up for his friend? Should he get a confessed murderer off in the first place? (One of my favorite moments as a playwright occurred during the Arizona State Theatre production. At intermission, while in the men's room, a total stranger who did not know I was the playwright turned to me and said, "Whatta ya think? The kid gonna get off?" Were we not both standing at urinals at the time I would've hugged him.)

In *Belmont Avenue Social Club*, a young guy, Doug, really wants a city council post, but the job goes to an old guy, Tommy. Doug is asked to prep Tommy for a press conference and finds out Tommy had a bogus rape charge against him forty years before. Now, the audience knows about Doug's ambition but Tommy naively doesn't. The final line of the act is, "I'll take care'a ya, Tommy."

The audience is now thinking, what's Doug mean by that? "Take care of him" and hide the charge? Or "take care of him" by stabbing Tommy in the back for his own political ambitions?

There is another cheap trick for getting out of the act, and that's the introduction of a new character. And if this new character does something intriguing to grab the audience's attention, even better.

In *Early One Evening at the Rainbow Bar & Grille*, a stranger, Joe, enters the bar in the midst of the apocalyptic craziness, seems to know the main characters (Shep and Virginia), and plays games with the phone. Then he turns to Shep and Virginia and says, "Down to business." Blackout.

This last bit of dialogue is an old-fashioned thing called a "curtain line." And it sets the audience off: Who is this guy? How does he know them? How did he get the phone to work when no one else could? (Or did he? We don't hear the other side of the conversation.) And what's he mean by "Down to business"?

Joe turns out to be God. So I gave him little bits of business to intrigue the audience, but not enough to tip the hand that he really is God, because if they know this at the end of the first act I had no second act.

And I found this out the hard way. In the early drafts, not only did Joe identify himself as God, the jukebox lit up and played the finale of "The Alleluia Chorus" and he was hit with a spotlight.

Great ending. Audience went nuts. Then the second act died. Why? No mystery. A guy comes in, says he's God, and the jukebox pulls a stunt like that: there ain't much doubt; this really is God.

So I changed it. Made his miracles tiny little things that any human could pull off. I also made him very calm, almost jovial, in the middle of the apocalypse—which in itself raised a question: Is this guy crazy?

Now, much of the second act was driven by the unanswered question of "Who is Joe?" God? Lunatic? Con man?

The first act ends with an unanswered question, and this unanswered question drives the second act. The audience put out their smokes and come back to have the questions answered. Without setting this stuff up, what's the point? Don't even try writing a two-act play without this step somewhere in your outline.

Something has to happen in the first act to make me come back and see the second.

Close your eyes and say it out loud ten times.

ANOTHER DRAMATURGICAL INTERJECTION

Bruce has given you a lot to think about in terms of shaping the question or questions of your play. Because I am a bit of a control freak, I like to encourage playwrights to embrace the idea of the outline.

It is relatively easy to write a short play based on some of the exercises suggested in the first chapter. However, when you are determined and driven to write a longer, full-length play, I truly believe that an outline can help you.

If each Roman numeral corresponds to a different scene or beat, you can begin to craft your play based on how a particular action might get accomplished.

Let's use my favorite play, A *Streetcar Named Desire*, as an example.

I. Blanche's arrival
    a. Surveys apartment and is disgusted
    b. Talks of past with Stella
II. Blanche meets Stanley
    a. Stanley suspect about Belle Reve
    b. Blanche drinks
III. Blanche meets Mitch
    a. Hope is promised
    b. Story of Blanche's first husband revealed
IV. Blanche and Stanley
    a. Hatred escalates
    b. Blanche's past revealed
    c. Rape occurs
V. Stella believes Stanley re: rape
    a. Blanche goes away
    b. Order is restored

This is all a little reductive, of course, but all Roman numerals and the subcategories are driven by an *action*. We are able to glean from the outline that the conflict of the play rests in the relationship between Blanche and Stanley and that Stella and Mitch serve as obstacles.

The key component to all this is that plays are rooted in action. Now, I know that there are many, many people who will argue this point with me. Chances are fairly high that those folks will not be reading this book.

There are plays that are driven by ideas, by images, by music, sometimes by chance. I love all these plays, but there is very little there that is quantifiable. You can't examine a hundred of them and see what goes into them. In "traditional" plays—with characters, dialogue, plot—you must have action. I beg you to please have some action.

As our good friend Isaac Newton tells us:

An object at rest tends to stay at rest and an object in motion tends to stay in motion with the same speed and in the same direction unless acted upon by an unbalanced force.

If you have a character at rest and no unbalanced force, you have no play. Plays, rooted in action, are born out of conflict. That should also be taped on every playwright's desk.

BRUCE'S PREWRITING

Now it's time for some prewriting. And this can actually be fun, because it's pretty mindless.

The secret here is to jot down every idea you get. Every idea. A line, a joke, a conflict, a costume. Don't worry that you haven't started act one and your brainstorm occurs in act two. Jot it down!

Fill up as many pages as you can. This gives you a kind of security blanket before you have to write the words "Act One."

One of the scariest things in the world is a blank page but now, thanks to all your prewriting, those pages aren't quite blank. It sounds crazy, but you'd be amazed how soothing this can be.

Let me map out how I do it. I've already done the first steps. Got my story. Got my act one climax. Now I know I can write the play.

After all of that, I can buy the notebook. Sounds crazy, but this is part of my ritual. Although I have dozens of half-filled notebooks around the house, a new play deserves a new notebook.

All my plays are written longhand. The notebook gives me more freedom while writing the play. Sitting at a computer screen makes me focus on that particular scene; sitting with a notebook makes me focus on the whole play. It's so much easier to throw in ideas, scribbled on the margins than to hit "Page Down" and type them in.

A notebook also gives you more freedom when it comes to where you want to write. I've written plays in bars (what a great excuse), while fishing, on trains, just about everyplace. So I have the notebook with me at all times. This is just a personal thing and if you're into typing that first draft, knock yourself out.

Okay, got the notebook. Now the next step for me is the music. Once again, this is strictly personal, but all my plays are written to specific music. Often this music makes its way into the play as either curtain music or—in the cases of *Belmont Avenue Social Club* and *Burkie*—as part of the actual play.

Like stretching before the marathon, music is part of my warm-up. It gets my brain thinking about the play before I even sit down to do that day's writing. I choose the music for different reasons, but it usually breaks down to character or tone/mood.

Burkie—Dixieland. Since death is a big part of the play I wanted something that could have a mournful quality, but also fought against that same quality. I used the bouncy/somber music of Preservation Hall Jazz Band.

Early One Evening at the Rainbow Bar and Grille—Nat King Cole. I wanted something lushly romantic, something from a different era that could actually be found on a small-town jukebox. This is the kind of stuff the character of Shep loved, so I used it.

Minor Demons and *Coyote on a Fence*—These are the only two of my plays that did not use curtain music and, ironically, I used the same music in writing both of them: Steely Dan. Cynical lyrics about death, drugs, and sex. Dark. Wailing sax. Perfect.

Moon Over The Brewery—Light, happy, nobody dies. The character of Miriam is a small-town artist with a touch of hippie about her. Figured she'd be a big Joni Mitchell, Carole King, Livingston Taylor fan.

Belmont Avenue Social Club—Sinatra. Lots of Sinatra. That was just the world of the play, and actually contributed one of the biggest laughs in the second act.

The Champagne Charlie Stakes—Although the story took place in the present, Charlie and Mary Lee lived in the past, so I used the music from their lives: Big Band.

Desperate Affection—This was a very dark (some say misanthropic) look at the male/female relationship. Like in *Burkie*, I wanted the music to play against the text; I wanted to set up an idyllic romantic situation in the audience's head, and then shatter it. Therefore I used lush Gershwin-like songs.

In the writing process, the music becomes almost like a mantra. After a while I don't even hear it, but I still want it there. However, if you have any sort of roommate it's important to be aware of their tolerance for this kind of music. (While I was writing *Belmont Avenue Social Club* my wife and I lived in rather tight quarters and, being broke, I only had one Sinatra tape, which I played endlessly. She finally kicked in the office door one morning, growling, "Buy another tape.")

Music also helps you work in places you wouldn't normally work. Put it in your car CD player and you'll think about it as you drive. Use headphones on an airplane, train, or subway to help you focus. Again, this is strictly personal. But I've found that any little thing that puts me into the world of the play helps.

One note on music: don't choose a piece because of specific lyrics. Many of my students will choose music because the lyrics help tell the story. Don't bother. It's a cheap shortcut and chances are the audience isn't listening anyway. I use music to put the audience, and me, in a certain mood.

Okay, you've come up with the plot, found some music, done your prewriting, have a fabulous first act climax. Now you can start the play, just as soon as you figure out who it is you want to tell your story.

3
CHAPTER

Writing Your Characters

QUICK, THINK OF YOUR FAVORITE PLAY. AND NO, CATS IS NOT A PLAY. I'M talking about good old, dull, straight plays. No chandeliers falling, no storming the Bastille.

Now think about your favorite movie. What is it you remember most about each? Chances are, in the movie it's the special effects or the action. In a play it's more likely to be the characters. Movies are story-driven. Plays are character-driven.

A DRAMATURGICAL INTERJECTION

I know that in the last chapter, I contradicted this statement. I think I even quoted Isaac Newton (which, trust me, I will do again). I believe that both statements can be true because characters *must have objectives*. An objective, says Mr. Stanislavsky, is an action.

LET'S RESUME

Because of the theatre's limited resources, your characters will probably become your greatest asset. If your characters are rich enough, plot and scenery take a back seat. Case in point: Albee's *The Zoo Story*. Two characters, a set consisting of a park bench and—and except for the final moments—no discernible action. And yet for almost sixty minutes Mr. Albee holds his audience because his characters, Peter and Jerry, are so fascinating.

Just about every character I've ever written has come from some place in my own background. On the rare occasions I've strayed from that, I had to immerse myself in research. And even then—as stated above with the first bike/*Coyote on a Fence* story—my own life sneaks back in.

Be warned though; there's nothing more boring than just writing about yourself. If you don't believe me, go see any Woody Allen film from the last few years. And as much as I may like many of Mr. Allen's early movies, they suffered from the author's own voice being interjected into all his characters. Don't believe me? Check out the dialogue in *Sleeper* or *Love and Death* and try to tell the difference between the voice of Woody and Diane Keaton. There is no difference.

Allen started as a stand-up comedian writing material for himself, and therefore was comfortable with his own voice. There is nothing wrong with that. When starting out, stay with what's comfortable, or as many others have said, "Write about what you know." To Mr. Allen's credit, however, he later learned to write non-Woody dialogue for other characters.

Let's talk about "voice"—a word we'll be using a lot in this chapter. I'm not talking about what comes from the larynx. I'm not talking about pitch, timber, volume, or singing ability. The voice is the thing unique to your character. A character's voice brings his entire life. His background, education, religion, age, sexual preference, geographic background, intelligence, personal taste, political bent, you name it. Every voice has a specific music.

Compare the character of Starbuck in *The Rainmaker* to Willy Loman in *Death of a Salesman*. Both are salesmen (albeit, Starbuck more of a con man) but they speak in a completely different rhythm. The words flow out of Starbuck; they come in fits and starts from Willy.

For starters, however, let's stick with your voice. What is it about the way you speak that makes you unique from the rest of us? If you don't know, you better start paying more attention. When Socrates (or the Oracle of Delphi) said, "Know thyself" he might as well have been talking about playwrights.

Listen to yourself. Do you speak in complete thoughts or fragments? Are you concise, or do you wander through your entire brain to make a point? Do you indulge in what I call "verbal hiccups"—those annoying little expressions that help us gather our thoughts: "like," "you know," "ummm," "know what I mean?" Do you have a regional accent? (Being from Philadelphia neither of us do, but the rest of you people sure have one.)

Creating the voice of the character goes hand-in-hand with the character's biography. This is a common acting technique but seems lacking when it comes to playwriting. An actor takes what the playwright gives him, and then fills in the blanks. If there's nothing about the character's childhood in the text, the smart actor makes it up, making inferences from what is in the text.

It's even more important that the playwright adopt this technique. The big rule when creating a character: Always remember that the character had a life before making an entrance.

In *The Champagne Charlie Stakes*, I had a character in his eighties. That means when Charlie enters he brings with him eight decades of history, all of which will affect what he says and does and how he relates to other characters.

Now is when you freak out and say, "Yo, I'm only a kid, how can I do something like this?" Well, hint number one: if you're really young and don't know any eighty-year-olds, don't write that character!

Wasn't that easy? I was in my thirties when I wrote that play, but I had a distinct edge: I knew the real Charlie for twenty years. Knew his family background, education, job history, musical taste, clothing taste, religion, what he did on Friday nights, favorite foods, commonly used expressions and other personality things. I was also well versed in his family relationships, which was what the play was all about.

And, pardon me for sounding abstract and "sixties" but I knew what Charlie's dream would be. By "dream" I don't mean what happens when you sleep. I mean, "If Charlie could've achieved anything in the world what would it be" dream.

You should always know what your character's dream is. Blanche DuBois wants to be swept away by a man (Mitch, the invisible Shep Huntleigh). Willy Loman's is to have his sons thrive in the business world, validating his role as father. Felix Unger, in *The Odd Couple*, wants to get back with his wife and return to his nice, neat apartment. Salieri's is to have the genius that comes so easily to Mozart.

In the above examples, the dream is an important part of the character. However, even when the dream is not vital to the play, you still have to know what it is. Our unfulfilled wishes are one of the things that drive us and characters in plays—at least the smart ones.

Charlie's dream was—for once in his life—to be a big shot at the racetrack. This was a case of the character's dream driving the play. Without that, no story. So make sure your character's dream is true to the character. A character without an organic, honest, and *focused* dream does not make any sense to an audience. How many times have you turned to a friend while watching a play and whispered, "Why doesn't she just *leave him*?" I contend that that is because the playwright did not do an adequate job of making us, the audience, keenly aware of what the character wants. I like to use the example from *My Fair Lady*: "All I want is a room somewhere, far away from the cold night air." Simple, direct, and instantly recognizable.

We now return to the creation of the character. What happens when you don't know anyone to inspire the character? Must you fall back on imagination? Not necessarily. In *Minor Demons* there is a character named Vince, a small-town police chief. Since I didn't know any small-town police chiefs, I did some research. I interviewed a couple of cops, observed people who were police officers, and learned the technical aspects of the job.

Now I can concentrate on the rest of his character. I wanted a guy with a chip on his shoulder; a guy who felt a little inferior. I thought back to a friend of mine in college who was the only Italian kid in a small coal town, much like the one in the play, and some of the prejudice he had to deal with. Having grown up just the opposite, in a predominantly Italian neighborhood with a lot of Italian friends, I latched onto this. I felt comfortable with the rhythms of the character because I had a whole street full of buddies to fall back on.

AN EXERCISE ON CHARACTER:
PREWRITING AND THE MONOLOGUE

Again, prewriting as a warm-up is a great idea when trying to find your character's voice. Often I will write a monologue that I have no intention of using. This way there's no pressure; it's between me and my notebook. I don't have to worry about keeping the audience's interest. Often it's just mundane ramblings, but in the midst of this the voice begins to emerge: his education, background, worldview, verbal hiccups.

Monologue writing is also a great way to experiment with how you tell a character's story. In monologues, one can find a way to articulate one's worldview (Think about Forrest Gump: his worldview is easily identified as "Life is like a box of chocolates.") or to reveal or discover something new (think about Nora at the end of A *Doll's House* and her revelation that she was, in fact, the skylark and the doll).

A DRAMATURGICAL INTERJECTION

I could make a case that there are three types of monologues:

1. A person telling an exciting story
2. A person discovering something *in that moment*
3. A person who has discovered something and is sharing it with another (or us, the audience)

Each one of these kinds of monologues will reveal a great deal of information about how a particular character might behave within the context of the play. Write one (or all!) of these monologues for each of your characters, thinking about the following questions:

1. Where do you begin?
2. Where do you wind up?
3. Who is the character talking to, and, more importantly, why?
4. How does this character talk?
5. How does this character move through ideas?

BACK TO BRUCE

On one occasion I wrote an entire one-act play as a warm-up. *Next Week, Spencer Tracy* was written while I playing around with the idea of *Burkie*. Knowing I wasn't ready to tackle a full-length play at the time I fell back on the one-act, a form with which I was much more comfortable. *Next Week, Spencer Tracy* dealt with six characters who gather once a week to watch free movies in a local park. (At the time I was doing this every Tuesday night. See? Everything is fodder for a play.)

Since the characters of Ed and Jon from *Burkie* were percolating in my head I decided to use them. I also used Janie, Ed's wife, who is not seen in *Burkie*. Ed and Janie stole the show. The loving, sometimes prickly, banter was right out of my parents' mouths and the audience loved it—especially Ed. This showed me a couple things:

1. Ed was an interesting enough character to carry a play. With some adjustments (mentioned above) I knew Ed's voice so well that replicating it would be easy.
2. I got a little practice on Jon. Since this character was very loosely based on me I needed to find out what I wanted to keep of my own voice and what I needed to invent. I did this by making Jon—in this play—shy, something I've never been accused of. His voice became tentative—a little unsure—some of which ended up in *Burkie*.
3. Although Janie never appears in *Burkie* she does play an important part in the story. And by putting her on stage, albeit in a comedy, I now had a clear picture of who she was.

Granted, writing an entire one-act play as a character warm-up might be a bit extreme but I was unsure whether my family (as characters) would work on stage. If nothing else, *Next Week, Spencer Tracy* gave me the confidence to write *Burkie*. And when you're starting out you need all the encouragement you can get. (After seeing *Burkie* for the first time my mother confided: "I like *Next Week, Spencer Tracy* better. I'm alive in that one.")

ANOTHER EXERCISE IN CHARACTER: CHARACTER WANTS

Take two characters. Let's call them A and B. A has the objective of trying to get a doctor's appointment. B has the objective of needing to tell A something important about the past.

Now answer the following questions:

1. What are the things that A needs to do to achieve the want?
2. What are the things that B needs to do to achieve the want?
3. What does each do to prevent the other from achieving their goal?
4. What does each do to allow the other to achieve the goal?

When we talk about a "character want," we also talk about rising stakes. If A does one thing in order to meet the objective, how does B respond? I'll ask you the vice versa, too.

The thing to keep track of, in this exercise, has nothing to do with achieving the want, but rather, the things that *this character might do*. What are the parameters of this character's will? Will A kill B in order to achieve the objective, if need be? Does B know the fine art of manipulation? Or is A a passive-aggressive sulker? Understanding behavior is key to understanding a character.

Pretend you're an audience member. You're sitting there, cell phone turned off, watching a play. Since very few theatres have curtains anymore you've already seen the set. What is it that captures your attention after that? With luck, it's the characters.

Every time a new character makes an entrance the entire audience focuses on that specific character. Who is that person? How's he dressed? What's he doing? What's his relationship to the other characters? Have we heard about him or is he a total stranger? Think back on plays with memorable characters. Chances are they had equally memorable entrance moments.

No matter what is happening on stage, the entrance of a new character always diverts the audience for a moment. Therefore, you really have to think about how you want that character to enter. As in life, fairly or unfairly, first impressions do count. And, also as in life, they do not have to be an accurate barometer of character, but they're usually pretty close. That's the first group we'll look at.

What I call the "true" character introduction is just that: an introduction that gives a truthful reading of the inner life of the character. By no means should it tell you everything you need to know, but it should make in indelible impression.

Take Stanley Kowalski. Please. (I love that joke.) Stanley enters, hollers up to his wife, Stella, then tosses her a blood-tinged package yelling: "Meat!"

Think about it. "Meat!" We the audience immediately realize that Stanley Kowalski is not a subscriber to the ballet. Mr. Williams wants to create a true modern primitive in Stanley, and he manages to achieve this impression within seconds of the audience meeting him.

On the flip side of that, recall the first time we see Blanche. She is dressed entirely in white, carries a suitcase, and is looking for directions. When she meets Eunice, her voice is, according to Tennessee Williams, "delicate and moth-like." After Eunice lets her into Stella and Stanley's apartment, we see Blanche find a bottle of whiskey and take a big gulp. This is a woman with a need for a drink.

Willy Loman slumps into his home late at night, exhausted. His first words: "I'm tired to the death." If that doesn't give you an indication of where this character's going may I suggest you take up accounting.

Although I don't like to cite too many movies, *Jaws* has one of the greatest introductions of characters ever: Robert Shaw as Quint, the shark hunter. The scene is a volatile town meeting. Suddenly, a SCREEEECH. We see a hand scratching fingernails against a blackboard. The noise causes the entire room to turn in that direction and go silent. Finally, we see Quint. Not only has he done the fingernail bit, he has added a comical chalk rendering of a shark eating a stick figure human. Now that the room is quiet, Quint waits a moment, takes a bite out of cracker, and finally speaks: "Y'all know me."

This is a great introduction of character. Not only is it theatrical, but within fifteen seconds we know a lot about Quint:

1. He has great intestinal fortitude. How many of us can scratch our nails across a blackboard without shivering?
2. He has a commanding presence in this town. The moment people see him they clam up.

3. He has a rather dark sense of humor. The shark cartoon's a bit distasteful since two folks have already been killed.
4. He is a supremely confident man. He keeps an entire room waiting for him to speak. Even takes a bite of a cracker.

Not bad for a few seconds of film.

"Lead" roles should not be the only ones to have "entrance" material. All of your characters should be given some sort of pizzazz when they step on stage. And sometimes it can happen when they enter not saying anything at all.

In Hecht and McArthur's *The Front Page*, we hear a lot about the character of Walter Burns all through Act One and ninety percent of Act Two. We even hear his voice barking over the phone, but we never meet him. At the end of Act Two the stage is crazy with action as approximately twenty characters scurry about.

As the act reaches its climax the characters all run off stage, and only now do we see Walter Burns, who immediately leaps into action, locking the others out. During the chaos he has snuck silently onto the stage, which is perfectly in keeping with the character; an amoral guy so intent on scooping the other reporters that he's not above a little chicanery to get ahead of the opposition.

In *Belmont Avenue Social Club*, I used everything but dialogue to try to establish the characters of Fran and Chickie. The published version of *Belmont Avenue Social Club* starts with a detailed description of the set. This is rare for me as I usually just give a general description. But I thought the look of the club was important so I spell out some specific things:

(Fran Barelli sits at his desk. There is a picture of Sinatra above it. Fran half-heartedly plays solitaire and mouths the words to the music coming from the tape player. Fran is in his late 50's: a heavy man but not flabby. Though not ostentatious, he looks like someone with money. Chickie Barelli, 40's, is at the pool table. They both wear suits. Fran's looks solemn; Chickie's is a few years old and a little flashy. Chickie is busy rolling the pool balls up and down the table, then following them with a videotape camera, attempting to film them. At first he tries just moving the camera, then repeats the procedure by actually walking and following the balls. He keeps alternating this procedure. Fran is facing away from Chickie. He throws down his cards, thinks a moment, makes a note on a small yellow pad, then opens one of the drawers looking for something. Chickie is still walking up and down the table filming the balls.)

Note: Neither character has said a word, but hopefully the audience, through costume and action, have a very basic idea of who they are.

Why no dialogue? I thought it was important to establish the club. Let the audience get acquainted with this room that is such a haven to the characters. Also, I had to take into consideration what happened before the play started. (Remember: your characters had a life before the eight o'clock curtain.) These guys have just come from the funeral of a good friend. People in a situation like this usually try to fill the time doing something mundane or comfortable. Had this been a normal day around the club, I probably would not have started the play this way.

Now I let Fran and Chickie speak. I wanted a quiet start to let the audience get to know these two guys in the first moments of the play.

FRAN: Yo, Chickie, didn't we have a file on . . .

> (*He finally turns to the pool table. Chickie is immersed in his filming, actually trotting next to the table.*)

What the hell're you doin'?

CHICKIE: Practicin'.

FRAN: Wha'?

CHICKIE: I'm not real good at followin' things yet. See, it's very complicated. I can't figure out which works better. Followin' it . . . (*He demonstrates*) Or just turnin' it.

> (*Again, he demonstrates as Fran looks through the desk.*)

See, if ya walk with it the picture goes up'n down. But if ya do this—(*He pans*) Then ya go too fast sometimes and ya miss what you're tryin' ta get. Very complicated.

Note: What I've tried to do here is introduce two very different characters. Fran is serious and very deep in thought about something. Chickie is not too bright. Their mode of dress is different. Chickie has a verbal hiccup: "Very complicated," which he uses to refer to very simple things.

FRAN: Didn't we have a file with pictures of all the guys?

CHICKIE: Wait'll Doug gets here. He'll know. (*Returning to his shooting*) Like at the cemetery this mornin'. I'm tryin' ta follow the coffin, right? But they get goin' down this little hill and start walkin' a lot faster—cause I guess Petey was startin' ta shift inside the box there—and I lost the whole thing.

FRAN: You really think that was smart?

CHICKIE: Wha'?

FRAN: Takin' movies of the funeral like that.

CHICKIE: So?

FRAN (*Patiently*): Some people might not think it's too, ya know, tasteful.

Note: Here I try to set up early the relationship between the two men. We find out later that they're cousins and Fran is protective of Chickie—and vice versa. Most people would not be so tactful with a guy that videoed a funeral.

CHICKIE: Ya think?

FRAN: I had Rose hangin' on my arm the whole time or I woulda' told ya.

CHICKIE: Don't worry. I'm gonna give her a copy.

FRAN: What's she wanta' copy for?

CHICKIE: 'Case somebody missed it. 'Case somebody wants ta see it again. I don't know. They do it at weddin's.

FRAN: Weddings are supposed to be happy, Chick. This was her husband's funeral. You really think she wants a tape of people cryin' their eyes out?

CHICKIE: So . . . I shouldn't give 'er a copy? That's what you're sayin'?

FRAN: Yeah.

What does the audience learn from the action? Hopefully, they see that this is Fran's domain; he is the man in charge. They also catch on to the fact he's a devoted Sinatra fan. Chickie? Well, Chickie's just not very bright. Therefore, he is quite content filming pool balls with various techniques.

The whole scene takes about a minute, but in it I try to let the audience know—through set, costume, music, and action—something about these characters and the day they've just been through.

A few minutes later I bring in another character, Cholly. Again, wanting to establish character quickly, I have the audience hear Cholly before he even comes on stage.

From offstage we hear:

CHOLLY (O.S.): Jesus Christ, will you turn off that fuckin' Sinatra?

> (*Cholly enters and moves directly to Chickie, not seeing Fran.*)

CHOLLY: Cut us a fuckin' break, will ya Chickie?

FRAN: You got somethin' against Frank?

> (*Cholly turns, surprised. His tone immediately changes.*)

CHOLLY: Hey Fran. Thoutcha' were still over with Rose.

FRAN: Whatta' ya got against Frank?

CHOLLY: Hey, Fran—you know me, I hate ta complain, right? It's just . . . if you're gonna pipe that out to the bar there can't ya play somebody different once in awhile?

FRAN: Who?

CHOLLY: I don't now. Somebody . . . different, ya know…maybe some . . . Tony Bennett. (*Fran snaps the music off*) Hey, don't turn it off—

FRAN: That's what ya wanted—

CHOLLY: Nahh, it's okay—

FRAN: It's off.

And what's the first impression of Cholly? He's foul-mouthed, irritable, and aggressive—with Chickie. When Fran steps into the fray he immediately becomes deferential. Cholly has the personality of a bully. His immediate retreat from Fran shows us this, along with underlining Fran's power.

Sometimes a character's lack of action tells us about him. In *The Champagne Charlie Stakes* I introduce four very verbose characters who are all comfortable with each other: Charlie, Mary Lee, Mary, and Jackie. They are waiting for an outsider to join the group, Mary's boyfriend Paul, who Mary has already warned us is kind of quiet. Paul is late to the racetrack because he's been attending his mother's funeral.

MARY LEE: How much did I win?

JACKIE: Forty, fifty cents.
> (*Paul enters. He's in his mid-40's, a serene looking man in jeans and a tee-shirt. He carries a metal canister and a bottle in a bag. He stands on the edge for a moment, looking unsure.*)

Note: It is not in Paul's nature to barge in on a conversation so I just have him stand there.

CHARLIE: 5-3-9! I don't believe it! I was gonna' play that.
> (*He shows Mary Lee his heavily marked form.*)

See it, honey? Got it right down there, 5-3-9. Got it right there.

MARY LEE: Along with about forty others.

CHARLIE: I was gonna' play it—

PAUL: Hi.

(*They all turn. Paul puts his things on the chair as Mary kisses him.*)

MARY: How'd it go?

PAUL (*A shrug*): Okay.

MARY: Are you all right?

PAUL: I'm fine.

Note: Paul, at this point, is almost monosyllabic. This is quite a contrast to the other characters and gives him a very different rhythm.

(*Charlie moves to him, shaking hands.*)

CHARLIE: Glad you could make it, Paul. Sorry about your mom.

PAUL: Thank you.

CHARLIE: Didn't pay ta get in, didja?

PAUL: Yeah, I did.

CHARLIE: Didn't Mary tell ya ta mention my name? They'd of let ya in.

PAUL: She did, but I felt a little funny. It was only—

CHARLIE: They'd of let ya right in. (*Starts to move off*) Maybe I can get your money back. Who's gate ya use?

PAUL: Don't worry about it, Charlie. (*He hands Charlie the bottle*) Congratulations on your race.

CHARLIE: Hey, thanks. Yeah, that's somethin', isn't it? See the form? My name, right at the top there.

(*He puts on his glasses to inspect the bottle as Paul moves to Mary Lee.*)

PAUL: Nice to see you again, Mary Lee.

MARY LEE: I'm so sorry about your mother.

PAUL: Thank you.

MARY LEE: This is our friend Jackie.

JACKIE: Hey, how ya doin'? Sorry 'bout your mom.

PAUL: Thank you.

CHARLIE: Hol-lee cow! Lookit what Paul brought me. Dom Perignon! (*To Jackie*) What'd I tell ya? This guy's successful. Whole chain'a bicycle stores.

PAUL: Just three—

MARY: Don't bother correcting him.

MARY LEE: Charlie multiplies everything. Except his age.

CHARLIE: Boy that's the truth. I'm the biggest b.s. artist ya ever met. But I'm honest about it.

MARY: Want something to drink?

PAUL: No, actually I was looking for—

CHARLIE: Jeeez, this musta' cost'a fortune.

Note: *Although Paul is the focus of this scene it is everyone else doing the talking. Poor Paul can't even finish a sentence. On stage, when a character has three other characters talking to him, his attention is pulled back and forth.*

CHARLIE: I gotta' tell ya though, Paul, I wouldn't know the difference. Too many years of the cheap stuff. I'll put this on ice, you kids can drink it during my race. (*Opens the cooler*) How bout some of the cheap stuff? Got a bottle in here with your name on it.

PAUL: No thanks. I really just—

Note: *Paul just wants to find a men's room but he's too polite to interrupt.*

CHARLIE (*Noticing the canister*): Brought your own, huh? Hey, I like this guy. Lookit the size of his flask. (*Shaking the canister*) Whatta' ya got in here, Paul? Some nice gin and tonics or somethin'?

PAUL: Ahhh…that's my mother.

> (*Charlie stops shaking it as Mary shoots him a look. There is a brief moment of awkwardness, and then Charlie speaks to the canister.*)

CHARLIE: Hiya, honey, how ya doin'? I'm Charlie, this is Mary Lee. Think she'd like a little champagne in there Paul?

> (*Paul just laughs, shaking his head.*)

Notice, Paul has very few lines, but it's the action swirling around him that tells us about his character. Soft-spoken, a bit shy, he's overwhelmed by the other characters, yet at the same time seems to enjoy them. Most people might be put out when someone mistakes their mother's cremation urn for a flask, but Paul finds the humor in it.

Remember, it's not just how your character acts that tells us about him; it's also how a character *reacts* to others. A more aggressive character than Paul would've acted very differently in this scene. He waits on the fringe, taking everything in before finally speaking. And even then, unlike the other characters who love to talk, he speaks in short bursts. Paul has a completely different rhythm compared to the other characters.

These are examples of first impressions that give a truthful glimpse of the character. However, this isn't always the case. The first impression the audience gets does not have to hold true for the entire play. I suppose we could call this the "misleading" introduction.

When we meet Regina in Lillian Hellman's *The Little Foxes* she is a charming, flirtatious hostess to her dinner guest, Mr. Marshall. Once Marshall leaves, however, the mask comes off and we see the real Regina—a rather treacherous woman. But if Regina is played correctly, we should not see this side of her until about page twenty. We should be as charmed with her as Marshall was. In fact, Regina's charm is one reason she's so good at being ruthless. The duplicity is a big part of her character, and for the audience to realize it they should be taken in, too.

Once again, this slow reveal mirrors life. Ever been stabbed in the back by a good friend? If you'd known this person had that quality they probably would've never achieved the title of "good friend." Therefore, you must have either not been perceptive enough to see this side, or the friend was really good at hiding it.

One of the cardinal rules of playwriting is that you must love your characters. (This is also true for actors.) If a producer called me, offering me big bucks to write a play about Hitler, the first thing I would do is find out the positive things in his character. We all know the monster side of him; I would have to find something else. For one thing, it would make him much more interesting, and therefore a more compelling character to watch. But more importantly, Hitler loved Hitler, so I have to find the side he loved and make that clear to the audience. Otherwise we have the same old character we've seen a million times.

It's especially important for the playwright (not necessarily the audience) to love the characters that are the least lovable, or you're probably writing a cardboard stereotype. I'm presently researching a play in which Al Capone is a character. In my story, however, the gangster is secondary to the opera-loving guy who opened soup kitchens for the poor and agonized over his partially deaf son.

I love plays where my loyalties are jerked around by the characters. Take *Glengarry Glen Ross*. Fifteen minutes into that play you're not sure who you're supposed to be rooting for. After a while, I just started rooting against certain characters. My loyalties are constantly shifting. To me, that means exciting characters.

I've used this "misleading" technique a few times in introducing characters. In other words, I let the audience think one thing about the character, but as the play moves on we find that first impression wasn't entirely true.

In class I'll often ask the question: Whose play is it? By this, I mean what character do we follow to the end? Which journey are we about to embark on? In *Belmont Avenue Social Club* I introduce Fran, Cholly, and Chickie. At this point the audience is wondering whose play it is. Which character are we rooting for? (Both are questions every playwright has to ask before putting pen to paper.)

Then Doug enters. I have Doug enter in the middle of one of Cholly's tirades. Remember, Cholly is the guy who said, "I hate to complain" but he proceeds to do that very thing throughout most of the play.

> (*Doug Reardon enters and stands in the doorway a moment, observing Cholly. Doug is in his mid-30's and dresses like a college professor.*)

CHOLLY: Hey, you know me, I back the police.

Note: "You know me" is Cholly's verbal hiccup.

But this asshole wastes half my day so he can finish his fuckin' paperwork. Fuckin' cops . . .

DOUG: Who's balls ya tryin' ta bust now, Cholly. Yo, Chick. Hey, Fran.

FRAN: How ya doin', Doug?

CHOLLY: Some wiseass cop over onna' west side. They call me about my truck. I told ya about my truck, right?

DOUG (*Smiling at Fran*): Couple times, yeah.

Note: I set up earlier that Cholly has told this story a few hundred times. Doug's smile is a little conspiratorial moment between him and Fran.

CHOLLY: Well, I want somebody's fuckin' head, I'll tell ya. Some nigger rips off my truck and whose balls do the cops bust—mine!

DOUG: If you saw the guy stealing your truck why didn't you stop him?

CHOLLY: I didn't see 'em.

DOUG: Then how'd you know he was black?

The first thing Doug does is bust on Cholly, heretofore the most obnoxious character on stage. Ahh, says the audience collectively: this is the hero! Then he jumps on Cholly's racism; Doug must be the guy in the white hat. Hooray! Doug the good liberal, friend of the black community, especially Wesley, a possible rival. I even make a point to have Doug dress differently than the rest.

Now the audience settles in smugly, assuming they are one step ahead of the playwright. (This is something very important: the audience is *always* trying to stay ahead of you by guessing the story. This is why twists and surprises are important.) By the end of the first act, however, they become uneasy. Doug, our good guy, might not be so good after all.

And then, in the final moments of the play and under Fran's prodding, I pull off his mask completely.

DOUG: Don't stand here and tell me you're givin' that seat to Wesley.

FRAN: He's not qualified?

DOUG: I didn't say that—

FRAN: I think he's qualified—

DOUG: Fran—

FRAN: Hell, you went ta Penn State. Wesley went to Princeton—

DOUG: Listen ta me—

FRAN: He's in—you're out—

DOUG: Bullshit—

FRAN: Oh yeah?

DOUG: You're not givin' it to him—

FRAN: Why not?

DOUG: You can't—

FRAN: Why not?

DOUG: You know why—

FRAN: You tell me—why not?

DOUG: You just wouldn't—

FRAN: Why not?

DOUG: You just wouldn't!

FRAN: Why not?!!

DOUG: He's a nigger! And there's no way in hell you're givin' that seat to a nigger so cut the bullshit!

This is very different from the Doug we met earlier; the one who busted on Cholly for his racism. The evil side did not emerge suddenly here; I begin to set the dark side of Doug up at the end of act one. Had Doug been a great guy through the whole play, only to change in the final two minutes, the audience would never buy it. You have to layer these things in.

Now, lest you think the misleading intro can only be used for the bad guys, I also use it for two of the nicest characters I've ever written: Tommy Krueger and Warren Zimmerman. Tommy's entrance in *Belmont Avenue Social Club* is less than auspicious. He's drunk. His eyes are red from crying. His suit is torn and dirty. And he has to take a leak. Naturally, this galls Doug since Tommy is the guy Fran has selected over him. And for a moment the audience agrees with Doug; Doug should get the job, not this old drunk.

However, in the second act we meet a much different Tommy. Tommy's not a habitual drunk; the reason he was loaded was because he was mourning his best friend, Petey. His suit got dirty in a fall while visiting Petey's grave. When sober we see that Tommy is a bright, gentle man who would actually make an excellent choice for the councilman's position. Now the audience isn't sure. The better Tommy looks, the worse Doug looks—and wasn't Doug the guy we were rooting for?

Warren Zimmerman in *Moon Over The Brewery* follows a similar course. When Warren is introduced he appears to be a bit of a boob. He stammers and has a funny laugh. He can't seem to match wits with Amanda, a thirteen-year-old girl. I even make a point to have him look sort of ridiculous; Warren's a mailman and I put him in the shorts and black knee socks uniform. With apologies to those fine folks at the Postal Service, that outfit makes anybody look a bit clownish.

As the play goes on, though, we find out that Warren's initial ineptness was caused by his own innate shyness. Warren's really a much more complex guy than his introduction would indicate. (At least I think so. Warren is one of my favorite characters.)

Introducing your character is a great way to plant—whether "true" or "misleading"—an impression with the audience. Figure out what you feel is the most important aspect of the character, then try to find an action to coincide with his entrance.

There's a wonderful scene in the film *Sexy Beast*. A married couple, already established as rather rough-edged, wait for another couple. When the other couple arrives it's clear they're both very upset. The wife tells the reason for their obvious consternation: "Don Logan called."

Now everyone at the table seems paralyzed by fear, just at the mention of "Don Logan." I don't know about you, but I can't wait to meet this Don Logan.

This is a great example of setting up a character before the audience even gets to meet him. And it's one of the oldest tricks in the playwriting book: Have other characters talk about him before he makes his first entrance.

Once again, this has its roots in reality. How many times in life have you heard about a person and then actually met them. Was the picture you formed in your head accurate? Most times, unless the person conveying the story is a complete idiot, it's pretty much in the same ballpark. The secret is to not make this dialogue sound like what it really is: character exposition.

A DRAMATURGICAL INTERJECTION

Not that Bruce is a complete idiot, but I think, with playwriting, you should also be thinking in terms of contradictions. What happens if the person doing the describing has something against the unseen individual? Why would one character talk badly or ill of another? How is that received by the audience—and when do they know it? If, as is the case in Susan Glaspell's famous one-act *Trifles*, one character completely discounts what another character is saying—to their detriment—what happens to our perception of character?

I am a big fan of perception, reversal, and unexpected behavior in characters, so long as you remain clear of what the "rules of the character's world" are. And that, again, means knowing what behavior this character could *potentially* display.

Now, you've done all you can to set up your character by having other characters discuss her. You've given her a memorable entrance. Now that she is on stage, what do you do with her?

This is where your character "want" comes into play. A character needs a reason to come on stage. Yes, you can say, "But she lives here. She's just coming home." And that's fine in real life but pretty boring in theatre. What does she want when she gets home? A drink? To use the bathroom? To be left alone after a rotten day? All of the above?

You must know what your character wants at every moment in the play. Not only does this drive the play or scene, but it drives your character. And characters react differently to situations when they want something.

In class I often use the door example. Some nefarious fiend has locked us in and it is imperative we get out. Being a disparate group each of us takes a different action. One pulls out a cell phone to call for help. Another tries to climb out a window. The third decides to set off the sprinkler system in the hopes the fire department will rescue us. One attempts to remove the hinges with a screwdriver from his Swiss Army Knife. And finally, the Stanley Kowalski in the group picks up a chair and tries to beat the door down. All are viable answers to the problem at hand: How do we get out of the room? But each character approaches the problem in a different way.

Even if there is no such scene in your play (and I hope to God there isn't) you have to know which option your character would take. Are they the Swiss-Army-Knife type or the scream-out-the-window type?

Characters have two levels of "want" that you need to familiarize yourself with: the *objective* and the *super objective*. If you have any acting training you're probably familiar with these terms. If not, here goes:

1. The objective—The immediate thing that your character wants. It can be simple: "I want a glass of water." Or, more complex: "I want you to have dinner with me." A character's objective often drives a scene.
2. The super objective—This is what its name implies: a *bigger* objective. In some cases it is the character's "dream," mentioned earlier.

In *Equus* the character of Dysart is a child psychologist assigned to find out why a boy has blinded six horses. That's his objective: solve the mystery and cure the boy. That's the immediate, surface-level "want."

However, Dysart is also a character on the edge himself. He's sleepwalking through his life, work, and marriage. Deep down, he wants to find out why this kid has all the passion that Dysart's now missing. In curing the boy, Dysart is trying to diagnose the problems in his own life. That is his super objective.

Every objective does not have to have a super objective attached. Perhaps your character wants a drink of water because he's thirsty, not to put out the fires of some traumatic childhood memory. However, good plays go beyond the superficial immediate objective.

Blanche DuBois's objective: a husband. Super objective: security and protection from all the ugliness in the world.

Hamlet's objective: avenge dad. Super objective: get uncle out of mom's bed.

Willy Loman's objective: prod Biff into being a business success. Super objective: validate Willy's life and beliefs by being successful.

Our students get sick of hearing us carp about the character "want" but in emerging playwrights' work, it is often the thing missing, to the detriment of the play.

The "want" is a combination objective and super objective. The character "want" is what drives the play. So if you're starting your script and don't know what it is your character wants close the notebook or turn off the computer because you do not have a play yet.

BACK TO BRUCE

One rule I have always found true, especially in my own work: The stronger the "want" the stronger the play. Let's look at three of what I consider my "better" plays.

In *Belmont Avenue Social Club* Doug really wants to be appointed councilman and will do just about anything, including going up against his mentor and destroying Tommy, a basically decent guy, to get it.

In *Desperate Affection* Maddie desperately (hence, the title) wants to make her relationship with Richard work. To do this she's willing to overlook that fact that he's a killer.

In *Coyote on a Fence* John really, really, really (no, really) wants Bobby to fight his scheduled execution. He also wants Bobby to show some remorse to help John write an obituary. And, last but certainly not least, John wants to permanently call off his own execution. That's three pretty strong "wants."

Now, let's look at one of the "lesser" plays. In *Early One Evening at the Rainbow Bar & Grille* Shep is a nonactive character. The coming apocalypse has filled him with inertia. The minor characters all voice stronger, more active "wants" than the protagonist. When Virginia enters, the play picks up because she's got a pretty strong "want" but when she finds out it's unattainable she drops it. Finally Joe/God enters and he does have a strong want. The only problem: we don't find out till the second act. Since *Rainbow* was an early play it's taken me quite a few years to realize that Shep's lack of a strong "want" was a major problem with the first act. Many have pointed out that the play "really starts" when Virginia enters. This is because until that point, the audience is a little confused as to what Shep's up to.

Rainbow is an example of what not to do. Avoid inert characters and don't introduce the "want" too late in the play. This said, you do not have to state it the second he steps on stage. Doug, Maddie, and John don't reveal their "wants" until twenty minutes or so into the play. Waiting until the second act, however, is pushing it.

ANOTHER DIGRESSION

I am one of a group of credited writers on the animated film *Anastasia*. While working on the script the "want song" became extremely important, since we really couldn't write the script until we knew what Anya wanted. Our songwriters, the very talented Lynn Aherns and Steve Flaherty, came up with numerous versions until the right mixture of both song and character "want" was achieved. Only then could we really concentrate on the story.

A character's "want" does not have to be one thing. In fact, during the course of the play, it might even change to something else. Hecht and McArthur's *The Front Page* is one of my favorites. As the play begins, reporter Hildy Johnson "wants" to get out of the newspaper racket, marry his fiancée and settle down in Philadelphia. This drives most of the first act. His editor, Walter Burns, has an equally important "want"—to keep Hildy in Chicago working on the paper. A jailbreak throws Hildy's plans off, and now his immediate "want" is to get the scoop and write the big story. Although his fiancée is still there in the background as a ticking clock, ("The train for Philadelphia is at six o'clock.") Hildy's "want" has changed, and that's what drives the play.

In case you haven't figured out by the extreme length of this chapter, we feel characters—interesting, quirky, lovable, infuriating, sexy, funny, sad, complicated characters—are perhaps the most important component to your play. Without them, what's the point? You're asking your audience to sit there for two hours with people on stage who don't hold any interest.

MORE EXERCISES IN CHARACTER

The Obituary

Find an obituary that interests you. It cannot be someone famous. Hopefully it's not your own. (I give my students a couple weeks notice before making them write this assignment. Sometimes it takes a while to find a really interesting one.)

Look at all the other information a good obituary might offer: age, geographical background, marital status, children, religion, education, military service, employment history. A lot of your background homework is already done. Hopefully, you begin to draw mental pictures of the people.

Now find one that sparks something in you. Some examples:

a. An unusual hobby or occupation
b. A family relationship
c. A "dream"—either fulfilled or unfulfilled

Once you choose your obituary focus in on that thing that sparks you and create a monologue based upon it. Before you do, however, get out your calculator and do a little math.

Let's say you've chosen Cordelia Smith, who recently died at the age of eighty-four. You chose her because she gave birth to quintuplets and you think this could make for an strong monologue if she talked about it the day after it happened.

She was thirty-two when this event occurred. Assuming she passed away in 2006, that would mean Cordelia was born in 1922. She lived through the Depression and World War II. It also means her quintuplets were born in 1954. That's when your monologue takes place.

You have to be very careful to make sure you stay true to both the character and the time frame. Different generations used different expressions and slang. I recently had a student writing a scene from the fifties use the expression "power walking." To the best of my knowledge, this expression was born in the 1980s. In *Burkie* I have Ed use the terms "gin mill" and "V-J Day." When's the last time you heard young folks bandying about these expressions? But for a man of his generation, they were quite natural.

In other words, you can't have Cordelia on her cell phone as the scene starts. If you're writing a scene that takes place in 1954, please do a little research. Who was the president? What kind of music was popular? If you're writing a scene that takes place in 1954 you should be careful to make the audience feel the time period.

One student of mine recently wrote a monologue that took place in the 1940s. He wrote the line, "Gimmie one of those desert horses." When I asked him to explain it, he told me he went on a web site looking for 1940s slang. "Desert horse" meant Camel cigarette. Needless to say, he got a pretty good grade on his project.

This lesson has brought forth some interesting monologues. One student found an obituary about a man who was a failed mink farmer and wrote a darkly funny monologue wherein the character speculated about what went wrong, all the while raking up a field full of dead minks.

Another chose a rather tall man for whom the highlight of the year was Halloween. He would dress up in an elaborate Frankenstein costume and scare the kids when they came up for candy. This monologue dealt with how the deceased tried to convince his teenage kids how "cool" he was for doing something like this, all the while putting on his very detailed costume.

One wrote a colorful scene about a man who dreamed of being a magician and playing the big casinos. (His relatives attested to the fact that this guy wasn't very good. He even had trouble with card tricks.) This man's idols were Siegfried and Roy. The monologue dealt with his Siegfried & Roy obsession while he performed a really awful series of magic tricks.

By their own admission these students all swore they would have never come up with these characters. Each of the scenes took some research: minks, Frankenstein, Siegfried & Roy. And all of them had some action, which is important for a monologue. Dealing with dead minks. Putting on makeup. Doing lousy magic tricks.

This exercise, because much of the background is provided for the character, allows you to concentrate on just the dialogue. But beware: you'll probably have to do a little research.

Waiting for a Character
This is fairly simply and straightforward exercise.

Characters A and B are on stage. They should be in the middle of a bargaining scene, but during the scene they also talk about character C. Character C should be there any moment. For some reason, A and B have differing opinions about C.

Once the character of C has been established by A and B, bring C on. Give C some sort of memorable entrance: he's arguing with someone on a cell phone, he's carrying a bunch of balloons, he's breathless from being chased by someone, he's wearing a dress.

Leave C on stage long enough so that we can see whether A or B had the more accurate opinion of C.

Observing from Photos
This was an exercise I designed when asked to speak to my daughter's second-grade class to get them thinking about characters and dramatic situations.

I took old *Life* magazines and cut out what I thought were interesting looking people doing unusual things. One was of a very intense looking young man speaking to the police. Another showed a man wearing a suit and riding a bicycle—in a dining room. (The former was actually taken from a bank robbery in progress—the basis for the film *Dog Day Afternoon*.) And another was a scene from a British play.

And there were others. One showed a Shriner in a tiny car. One showed a huge, rather nasty looking woman in her garden. One showed a sad looking woman staring out the window on a rainy day. I cut out sixteen different pictures, backed them with cardboard, numbered them, and lined them along the wall.

The kids were given a sheet with questions about the characters: name, age, occupation. Were they angry, scared, happy, lonely? What about the situation itself? Why was the man riding a bike in the house? Was that man helping the police? Why was that woman in the garden so mean-looking? Then they were asked to choose one and explain what they thought was going on in the picture. They had to give the character a name and tell me something about him/her.

Characters turn up in the oddest of places. All you have to do is pay attention.

4

CHAPTER

Creating Action, Dramatic Tension, and Bargaining

WE'VE TALKED A LOT ABOUT WARMING UP, OBSERVING THE WORLD, OUT-lining a play, and creating characters. However, all this work is utterly useless if there is no conflict, no action, or no tension. Remember that our good friend Aristotle put "plot" (and that means action!) ahead of character in his *Poetics*. If you don't have action, you don't have a play.

A good part of action involves "bargaining," a phrase we both use in class. And no, it has nothing to do with a student attempting to get a better grade. In a bargaining scene, two (sometimes more) characters all want something. The bargaining occurs when we see how they go about it. Basically, it's how a character accomplishes—or doesn't accomplish—his want. (In his excellent book *The Dramatist's Toolkit*, author Jeffrey Sweet calls this a "negotiation.")

The character you create will determine what type of bargaining occurs. Aggressive characters bargain differently than passive ones. Intelligent characters bargain differently than less-than-intelligent ones.

In *Long Day's Journey into Night*, the Tyrone brothers both want their father's whiskey. Edmund gets it by playing on his father's sympathy, a very passive act. Jamie, on the other hand, has tried to pick the lock that keeps him from the booze. So aggressive has he been that the lock is actually scratched from his efforts. These are two very different ways of getting the thing they want. And both actions are perfectly in character. Edmund bargains. Jamie attacks. Edmund gets the whiskey with his father's blessing; Jamie is defeated by the lock. Two different bargaining styles. Two different results.

Sometimes a character will change tactics when one doesn't work. In *Macbeth*, Lady Macbeth goes through a whole series of tactics to get what she wants.

First: What does she want?

Objective: Get her husband to kill King Duncan.

Super objective: Kill Duncan to fulfill prophecy making Macbeth King and her Queen, satisfying her lust for power.

So, how does she get her husband to commit murder? Two steps. Step one: reflections on his manliness.

1. Accuse him of cowardice: "And live a coward in thine own esteem . . ."
2. Attack his manhood: "When you durst do it then you were a man . . ." Here, she states clearly that she is the tougher of the two: "I would have, while it was smiling in my face, have plucked my nipple from his boneless gums and dash'd the brains out had I so sworn as you have done to this . . "

Okay, now she has made him nervous.

I would also note that our good friend Shakespeare has given Lady M the ability/gift/insight to challenge her husband on his weakest points. We learn early in the play that there is an "heir" question, as well as some assumption that, while Macbeth was heroic in battle, others were somewhat more heroic. She does not dance around with assertions that might make him slightly uncomfortable; she cuts to the heart of his person and psyche, which tells us that she knows him extremely well. We can also imagine that she has "encouraged" him to do one or two other things in their shared past. Shakespeare's wisdom in creating this character is born, I would argue, out of his close observation of people (remember the airport?) and relying on traditional notions about men and women. I'll talk more about that in a bit.

Step two: convince him he'll get away with it.

1. The plan: Get Duncan's guards drunk: "His two chamberlains will I with wine and wassail so convince that memory, the warder of the brain, shall be a fume . . ."
2. Not only will we get away with it, we can frame someone else for it: "His spongy Officers who shall bear the guilt . . ."

Lady M's bargaining makes perfect sense. Soften up husband by slurring his manhood and getting him leaning toward the plan. Once that occurs, convince him with the final argument that not only will they not get caught, they can pin it on Duncan's guards, slay them, and look like heroes.

A couple of things make this a brilliant scene:

1. The bargaining is part of the plot. If Macbeth doesn't kill Duncan, there's no story.
2. The bargaining seems real. Talking your spouse into killing royalty is not something one does every day; it's a rather unbelievable situation. Yet, by pushing all the right buttons emotionally and rationally, Lady M succeeds.
3. The bargaining stems from a very strong "want." The stakes are pretty high in this scene. This is not a scene about who takes out the garbage. (Or even a scene about who gets the whiskey, although in O'Neill's family that alone was pretty high stakes.) This is about murder and seizing control of a country.

In the above two examples, there is a clear-cut winner. The Tyrone boys get the booze; Macbeth commits the murder. In theatre, as in life, however, this is not always the case.

In order to have a bargaining scene, there must be some dramatic tension on stage. Unless a character has that "want" there's nothing to bargain for. In a full-length play, that character want can drive your story, but along the way there will be other, smaller wants that will call for bargaining. And these little dramatic tensions along the way keep your audience's attention while you're layering in the main story.

Again, *Glengarry Glen Ross* is a great example. The overall "want" for the characters is to get the new customer leads. During the course of the play, however, there are dozens of other "wants"—all of which require bargaining. Ricky and the reluctant customer. Moss wanting George to break into the office for him. Shelley trying to bribe John, the office manager, for a look at the leads.

Again, each character uses a different method of bargaining. Moss uses mutual anger with a tinge of bullying. Ricky uses charm. Shelley uses money. If the whole play were simply "we-want-the-leads," it would get old pretty fast. It's these little dramatic-tension-bargaining scenes that keep us interested.

In the first act of *Burkie* I do a lot of tap dancing to keep the audience interested until the main conflict kicks in. I use some bargaining scenes, but since

I'm also trying to force-feed the audience some exposition I try to work that in, too.

Early in the first act I have back-to-back bargaining scenes. While reading them, see what exposition I try to sneak in, both facts and inferences.

The scene is the Burke home, late afternoon. Jon is in the kitchen. Ed sits in the living room with a box of trophies. (This scene has been shortened from the original.)

ED: Hey, Jon. Bring me in some of that tarnish remover crap. Under the sink.

JON: What're you workin' on?

ED: Brought down some'a your sister's old trophies.

JON: What for?

ED: She's got that big house now. Might wanta' take 'em home.
　　(*Jon enters with a rag and polish.*)

JON: I don't think so, dad.

ED: Why not?

JON: People in Phoenix don't have fireplaces and mantels. Where'd she put 'em?

ED (*Holding up a trophy*): 'Member this one?

JON: Dad . . .

ED: What?

JON: Jess just . . . she's not into this sorta' stuff.

ED: Yeah . . . well, anyway I gotta' start getting' rid of some of this junk. Ya accumulate a lotta' stuff in thirty-five years. That attic's loaded.

JON: I know.

ED: You're mother's the one. That woman wouldn't throw away a thing. Kept every gift every student ever gave her. Whole carton of cards up there with "Mrs. Burke" on the envelopes. (*He holds up a trophy*) That was the big one. All star game.

JON: Uh-huh.

ED: 'Member that game?

JON: Yep. I also remember her taking the trophy out of the living room and hiding it down the basement.

ED: Yeah. I gotta' couple weird kids. (*Putting the trophy back*) You're late today.

JON: Little.

ED: You stop at Dom's gin mill there?

JON: I stopped at the bakery.

ED: What for?

JON: The cinnamon buns.

ED: Hunh? (*He looks confused for a moment*) Oh, yeah. That was nice. Your sister likes them. You got enough money on ya?

JON: Yeah, dad. I'm fine.

What have you learned so far from the exposition?

1. The first dramatic tension is tiny. Ed wants to put out the trophies but Jon thinks it's a bad idea.
2. The dialogue about the cinnamon buns also occurred a few moments earlier and Ed has clearly forgotten it. This is what propels Jon into the kitchen.

   (*During the course of this scene, Jon takes a container of pills and counts the contents as Ed rummages through the box in the other room.*)

ED: I got hockey, lacrosse, and basketball. Didn't she get somethin' for softball?

JON: Softball was summer. They didn't give trophies.

ED: Hey—here's your medal.
   (*He pulls out a tiny medal.*)

JON: What medal?

ED: That track medal ya won, 'member? I came ta see ya run. Rained like hell. You want this or not?
   (*Jon has finished counting the pills and crosses to the doorway.*)

JON: It was a fourth place medal.

ED: So?

JON: There were six of us in the race.

ED: Well, ya tried, didn't ya? Here's a plaque from that piano thing you were in—

JON: Why didn't you take your pill?

A few more observations and questions:

1. The rhythms will suddenly change with Jon's last line.
2. I've put in some director-proofing. This could have been a very static scene so I have incorporated action within the dialogue. It's impossible to do this scene without Jon counting and Ed polishing trophies.
3. What inferences can you derive about Ed as a father?
4. There are unanswered questions raised in this scene: What are Ed's health problems? Why did Jess hide her trophies down the basement?

JON: There were nineteen in here this morning, there's nineteen in here now.
   (*Jon moves to the kitchen for a glass of water.*)
ED: What're you—my keeper?
JON: It's not good to throw your medication off schedule.
   (*Jon crosses to him with the pill and water.*)
Here.
ED: I'll take it later.

Note: This is the first bargaining scene—observe how Jon manipulates Ed.

JON: You're eight hours late already. Now will you take this?
ED: Don't tell me what to do.
JON: I'm not telling you. I'm asking nicely. See? I'm even smiling. (*He forces a smile*) Now will you take your goddamned pill?
ED: Later!
JON: Now!
ED: Who the hell you think you're talkin' to?
JON: You're hurtin' already, aren't you? You're hot—you're rubbin' your head—
   (*He reaches out as if to feel Ed's temperature. Ed jerks away from him.*)
ED: I'm all right!
JON: You're not all right!
ED: How the hell would you know?
JON: Dad, please . . .
ED: I'm not takin' that stuff with your sister comin' up.
JON: Why not?
ED: I don't want her seein' me on that stuff.

JON: She knows you're sick—

ED: She don't know how sick. And I don't want her seein' me all doped up like that—understand?

JON: You know what happens when you don't take it. You want Jess to see you like that, huh?

ED: I haven't seen your sister in a year and I'm not gonna' sit around like some sorta' goddamned zombie!

> (*Jon stares at him a second, shrugs in resignation, and returns the pills. Ed follows him to the kitchen, but does not say anything right away.*)

Observe:

1. At the end of this first bargaining scene, Jon has lost. Ed's "want" is clearly stronger. It's also in character for both of them. Jon retreats, knowing how stubborn his father can be.
2. Another unanswered question that I pointed out earlier: what happens if Ed doesn't take the pill?
3. The rhythms change again, as they often do at the end of a bargaining scene.

ED: Damn, where the hell is she?

> (*Jon says nothing.*)

Probably sent her suitcase ta Canada or somethin'.

> (*He laughs; Jon does not respond.*)

What'd you have for lunch?

Observe: You don't always need dialogue to make your point. Jon knows what buttons to push on his father and is giving him the silent treatment. Ed responds by asking a direct question, therefore forcing him to respond.

JON: Tuna sandwich.

ED: Oh great. I ordered ya one for dinner.

JON: Don't worry about it.

ED: I'll call Dom—

JON (*A little louder*): Don't worry about it. (*He opens the refrigerator, pulling out a beer*) Tuna's fine.

ED: You gonna drink now?

JON: One of us oughta be medicated.

> (*He crosses to the living room loosening his tie*) Any mail?

We now move into the second bargaining scene.

ED: Oh, yeah. There was somethin' for ya.

> (*He finds the envelope.*)

That whatta' ya call it…that thing you go to in Boston.

JON: The competition?

ED (*Handing him the letter*): Yeah, that's it. Those bastards down the bank aren't gonna give ya hard time are they? It's just a couple days.

> (*Jon simply stares at it.*)

You gonna open it or what?

> (*Jon drops it in the trash can.*)

JON: Junk mail.

ED: Aren't ya goin'?

JON: Don't think so—

ED: Last year ya almost gotta' job outta' it.

JON: I have a job—

ED: A music job.

JON: Forget it, dad.

ED: Go on. Have some fun. Maybe you'll meet a broad.

JON: Women who go to piano competitions always look like they stepped out of *The Addams Family*.

> (*Ed retrieves it from the trash can.*)

Just leave it, huh? I couldn't go even if I wanted to.

ED: Why not?

JON: These people practice six hours a day seven days a week. I couldn't catch up.

ED: Ya might change your mind.

JON: I'm not gonna' change my mind. Throw it out.

ED: I really wish you'd go.

JON: That's a switch.

ED: Look, if you're worried about me—

JON: I'm not worried about you—

ED: You are too, don't gimmie that. And ya don't have ta be—it's stupid. Aunt Wilma's right down the street, she'll be stickin' her nose in the back door every five minutes. (*He holds the envelope out to Jon*) Come on. Open it.

JON: I'll make you a deal. I'll open the letter if you take your pill.

     (*They say nothing for a moment, then Ed drops the letter back into the trashcan.*)

ED: You couldn't be more like your mother if she spit ya right outta' her mouth.

I told you it was a lot of exposition. It also uses some of the devices we spoke about earlier, the most important being "talking about a character before she shows up." The audience is now anticipating something: the arrival of Jess, a new character. But before she comes on stage, they should have a mental picture of her because of the facts laid out by Jon and Ed.

As for the bargaining, nobody wins. Jon doesn't open the letter and Ed doesn't take the pill. By putting the exposition into a bargaining scene, we have created some dramatic tension on stage: one character wants something, the other doesn't.

Notice that the bargaining in these scenes involved props: envelopes and pills. But a bargaining scene doesn't have to be about "things." It can involve actions: vote for this guy, come out to dinner with me. It can involve thought: "Don't you agree with my opinion?"

BARGAINING EXERCISE 1

Pick two opposite characters: boyfriend/girlfriend, father/daughter, mother/son, boss/employee, cop/criminal, doctor/patient, salesman/customer. The list is endless. Now come up with a bargaining scene. What would a father/daughter have to bargain about? Salesman/customer? That's pretty obvious. Before you start the scene, however, tell yourself whom you want to win. Or—decide that neither wins.

Then map out four distinct levels of bargaining. Check out Lady Macbeth for an example.

Remember, you can never have enough dramatic tension or character "wants" in a play. And once you create them, the bargaining should come a lot easier.

SOME WORDS ABOUT ACTION
AND "DIRECTOR-PROOFING"

Before becoming a playwright I was an actor and, as such, often experienced "the actor's nightmare." For you civilians who have never trod upon the boards, let me explain. It is literally a nightmare wherein you are in a play, about to go onstage, but you have no idea what show you're in or what character you're portraying. It's a pretty frightening experience.

Now that I've been away from the greasepaint for quite a few years I've discovered something: there is a Playwright's Nightmare. It goes something like this: I arrive at a theatre to see a production of *Moon Over The Brewery*, which takes place near an old coal mining town in Pennsylvania. As the lights rise I see a set that looks like something out of the last plays of Tennessee Williams: a crumbling southern mansion complete with exotic plants and Spanish moss hanging from the marble columns.

I leap up and find the director at the back of the theatre and immediately grab him by the lapels, demanding an explanation. He tells me he decided to "change the locale."

At this point I wake up smacking my pillow around and screaming, "That's not the way I wrote it!"

Some plays are wide open to a director's interpretation or concept. Shakespeare is constantly reinvented. Plays that have an abstract quality to them, such as *Equus*, can change styles from production to production.

My ripoff of *Equus*, *Minor Demons*, can also be open to a director's concept. I saw it done with a massive production, including special effects, in Arizona. Off-Broadway it was done with six chairs. *Coyote on a Fence* also gives a director more freedom to explore a concept. But that's about as far as it goes with my plays because—for better or worse—they are "realistic." *Belmont Avenue Social Club* is a crappy little backroom with a pool table. Yes, you can get creative with the shade of the paneling or color of the felt on the pool table, but that's about it.

One of my other fears—besides the Spanish moss thing—is that a director will take my play, put characters in chairs, and just let them talk. No movement. No action. No pretty compositions. And so I always put what I have termed director-proofing into all my plays.

Director-proofing should do two things: give your actors something to do and your audience something to watch. Director-proofing is no more complicated than putting movement and action into your script. Remember, Aristotle talks about the "spectacle" of theatre, which means you have to give the audience something to look at. In practice, in my plays, I'm talking about small things. Actions you'd see in everyday life.

Think about it; how many times in life do we just sit and talk? We do other things: mix drinks, cook, clean, look for something. Even if we do just sit and talk there are other things going on: we put on music, pass around pretzels, look through magazines, channel-surf.

When outlining *Belmont Avenue Social Club* I realized the staging could become a bit stagnant, especially when all five characters were on stage at the same time. That's when I came up with the idea of the pool table. Now—unless the director is an absolute idiot—the actors have to *do something*. Automatically, there is movement on stage.

The best way to ensure you get the movement you want is to put it into the dialogue. Ed and Jon would look pretty ridiculous in the bargaining scenes if they just sat there. Ed has to polish trophies and Jon has to count pills because they actually talk about it.

A Streetcar Named Desire is filled with director-proofing; all the "action" scenes are also in the dialogue. Stanley explains the Napoleonic code and makes references to Blanche's jewelry while ransacking her trunk. The smashing of the radio, the tossing of the meat, are all incorporated into the dialogue so the action must be performed.

Director-proofing, if done right, also is a huge help to your actor. Most actors love action and props. The secret is to make sure the action or prop you give them is in character.

One of the most common problems new playwrights face is getting some "action" into their plays. By action I mean just that: physical action like fights, slaps, shootings, and stabbings. When we talk about those things, we immediately think about movies. And here's a simplistic statement: plays aren't movies. With new playwrights, the line between the two often blurs. (Another digression: a friend of mine raised in a small coal town saw his first play at the age of thirty-four, my *Moon Over The Brewery*. He grabbed me at intermission to let me in on his discovery: "There's *real people* up there!")

When new playwrights hear "action" in connection with any kind of story they tend to automatically think in terms of violence. There are, as we all know, other types of action besides car chases and shootouts. Sometimes, a character walking across the stage to pick up a note can say more about character and want than an entire backlot of stuntmen swinging from chandeliers. Remember, we are trying to create "real people up there."

The nice thing about theatre audiences is that they will occasionally use their imaginations. *Death of a Salesman* is all about...a death of a salesman. But we don't see the death—it happens offstage. *Hedda Gabler* shoots herself . . . offstage. Blanch DuBois is raped . . . after the lights go down.

These were all done for practical reasons. How can you stage Willy Loman's car crash? Do we want to see Hedda's brains blown across the stage? And isn't the image in your mind of Blanche's rape far more disturbing than what any director can stage?

Practicality aside, however—and more importantly—it works artistically. Now the audience becomes active in the storytelling process; the playwright has given them enough information to paint the picture of what happened.

If your play does call for a particularly violent act, think in terms of theatricality. Theatre is not a totally literal art that applies to action. For instance, the climax of *Equus* shows a young man, Allan, acting out the blinding of six horses. Does anybody want to see someone literally perform this? Do producers really want to deal with the PETA people?

Mr. Schaffer designs the final moments of the play as part of a ritual, which plays into the overall thought behind the play. He has six actors whose faces are visible wear stylistic horses' heads. At no time are they meant to resemble a horse, but the audience buys into it. Now this brutal act becomes almost balletic. No sharp object ever comes remotely close to a "horse," but the effect is mesmerizing.

Above, I referred to my play *Minor Demons* as a rip-off of *Equus*. (Remember, if you're going to steal—and when you start out, you should—steal from the best.) *Minor Demons* has a similar, albeit much smaller effect. In *Minor Demons* I had a father grab his son and shake him violently. Now, this is something we've seen on stage a million times, and the minute you realize that, start to think of ways around the cliché. This goes for anything, not just action; the moment something seems too familiar, try to approach it a different way.

Since the play was in the form of a dream (and therefore not "realistic") I had the freedom to try something different. So, I put the father on one side of the stage, the son on the other, and didn't even have them look at each other. They both stare out at the audience as they perform the scene, but then the father "grabs" the son (really just getting some empty air) and the son, thirty feet away, reacts—moving onto his toes, trying to ward off the blows.

If there is a "lesson" to be learned about action and bargaining, it comes from Volansky's good friend Isaac Newton, in his third law of motion: "For every action, there is an equal and opposite reaction."

What do you know when you see a bear chasing you? Unless you are Grizzly Man, you run in the opposite direction. Fast. What do you do if you are Blanche and Stanley is coming close to discovering your deep, dark secret? You deflect, react, and fight back. What do you do if you are Willie Loman and you've just been fired? You kill yourself to give your son the insurance money.

Characters, like those forces at rest and in motion, demand action.

5

CHAPTER

Structure

OKAY, LET'S START THIS IMPORTANT CHAPTER OFF RIGHT AND INVOKE A tired cliché, shall we? "Writing a play is like building a house. If the foundation is bad, it won't hold up."

We use clichés like this for a reason—they are true. Structure (closely related to Aristotle's "plot") is as pivotal to a play as the story itself. Imagine what would happen if Stanley raped Blanche in the third scene, and she met Mitch in the seventh. *Streetcar* would not be the brilliant play that it is.

As I mentioned earlier, I keep a folder full of newspaper clippings. It's my "maybe I'll write these stories someday" file. It's overflowing with yellowing articles. And so far I've only gotten two plays out of it: *Coyote on a Fence* and *Top of the World*.

What? Never heard of that second one? That's because it's only been produced twice—thank God.

I was intrigued with a story from Alaska. Three whales, somehow screwing up their own instincts, got stuck in a hole in an ice flow. International story. Worldwide effort to free these whales. Russians and Americans, natural enemies, link hands to try and rescue these, well, three really stupid whales. Now, I have nothing against whales. I cheer when Ahab gets his comeuppance. But come on, with all the problems in the world did we really have to put all this money and manpower behind an effort like this? Why are we doing this, I asked myself. The answer was simple. People like whales. If it had been three scorpions trapped somewhere we wouldn't see it on the front page, that's for sure.

Here, I thought, was a play. A wild comedy showing the government folly. I flew through the pages, getting even with everybody: politicians, environmental extremists, conservatives, liberals, television hosts—even the Pope. It was possibly the funniest thing I've ever written. And it was a lousy play.

Why? As William Saroyan says in *The Time of Your Life*: "No foundation. All the way down the line." All I had was a premise. No story. Just a jumping-off point. Don't get me wrong, I tried. I put in a character with a "want." He just wasn't very interesting and that's because I put him into the middle of a cartoon, which is tough to sustain for two acts in the theatre.

Without the foundation of a strong story—or character—I had nothing upon which to build. The second act became episodic and didn't rise. The stakes themselves, freeing the whales, just weren't interesting enough (at least the way I did it) to hold up a full-length play. Might've made a pretty good half-hour one-act or—more likely—a *Saturday Night Live* sketch, but I was a playwright damnit so that's what I did: Made it into a bad play.

A DRAMATURGICAL INTERJECTION

Sometimes, when I am feeling particular frustrated by a play, I find myself thinking about what might have gone wrong. Bruce is right when he asserts that without a strong foundation, there can be no sustainable play. The operative word here is *sustainable*. There are many plays that are smartly built, have compelling characters with strong wants and intelligent, logical dialogue. But they cannot sustain themselves over the course of an entire play. As I've said a million times, each moment and scene needs to build upon the next. What is the thread that connects each character and each action to the next? For me, it is all about the foundation, and making sure that the play tracks. It is why "internal logic" is a mantra to be chanted again and again.

BACK TO BRUCE

Then there was the story that inspired *Coyote on a Fence*. This had not only an interesting premise and intriguing character, it had stakes—life or death—high enough to support a full-length play.

As I look through this pile of clippings, I find only one other story that might offer a strong play foundation. The rest are just characters or incidents that may someday end up as a small part of a larger work. Two of the articles have made it to television: one as a half-hour film, the other as a four-minute monologue. Both of these shorter venues worked because the stories themselves were slight. They would have died had I attempted to base a play around them. Not enough foundation.

Before you begin to write your play, ask yourself some questions:

1. Is this story and character interesting enough to hold an audience's attention for two hours? Is there a really compelling obstacle your character must overcome? Does he have a strong "want"? Is it a "want" the audience will identify with?

2. Are the stakes high enough? Life and death are a pretty sure bet: *Burkie, Coyote on a Fence, The Crucible, As Is*. The pursuit of happiness and staving off of loneliness work: *Desperate Affection, Moon Over The Brewery, Glass Menagerie, A Thousand Clowns*. Pursuit of political power, sure: *Belmont Avenue Social Club, The Best Man, Macbeth*. A person's freedom: *Inherit the Wind, The Caine Mutiny Court Martial, Witness for the Prosecution, Twelve Angry Men*.

If the answers to questions 1 and 2 are "yes," you can continue writing. If not, start some serious rethinking.

More questions, from both the playwright and the dramaturg:

1. Is there an Aristotelian "thought" behind your play? In other words, you may have a ripping good yarn to tell, but will the audience take home anything else with them when the curtain comes down? One can look at *The Caine Mutiny Court Martial* as an intriguing courtroom drama but there's more there. The final scene wherein the character of Greenwald lets his true feelings known brings up all sorts of questions about war and the men needed to win it. But until that point it's just a really good courtroom drama. *Witness for the Prosecution*, although in the same courtroom drama category as *The Caine Mutiny Court Martial*, has no real "thought" behind it. It falls into the ripping good yarn category and it makes for a very entertaining evening in the theatre. What makes *The Caine Mutiny Court Martial* the better of the two plays is that one has that extra something special: a thought behind it.

2. Do conflicts and obstacles pile up on your character throughout the course of the play?

List them if that helps. Let's try our old friend Blanche DuBois.

1. Blanche arrives with no place to live and no money.
2. Stanley and Stella's apartment is already small and crowded, adding to the claustrophobia and tension as the play goes on. (If Mr. Williams put the Kowalskis in a spacious home the play would not have the built-in dramatic tension it does.)
3. Blanche meets Mitch and the audience sees a spark of hope for both of them.
4. Stanley suspects Blanche of ripping off Stella and ransacks her things.
5. Stanley checks out Blanche's sordid past and tips off Mitch, ruining that relationship.
6. Blanche, already fragile, is sexually assaulted by Stanley, finally pushing her over the edge and into a mental breakdown.

This is a pretty impressive list of conflicts and obstacles and proves a very important point when planning the structure of your play: if the curtain goes up at eight, by nine-thirty your main character should be in some hot water. In other words, as the play progresses, *make it rougher on your character*. You do this by putting obstacles in the road. In a properly structured play, these obstacles should get more and more challenging and the choices your character makes become more important in the long run.

A very general plot outline is a huge help before you start the play (remember that chapter?). There's nothing mystical about plot; it's just the order of events that occur in your play. Plot is probably the most logical piece in the whole puzzle of playwriting.

Let's look at the plot point list again. Blanche meeting Mitch (3) has to happen before Stanley can tip Mitch off about her (5). And plot point 1 has to happen before any of the others. This might seem elementary, but putting down all your plot points first provides a skeleton to which you can then add the meat. (There are always exceptions to the rule, of course. Pinter's *Betrayal* starts with the end of the play and then works backward. Even with this reversal of order, however, there has to be a logical progression. Instead of A leading to B, B now leads to A.)

Some plays are more plot heavy than others and therefore the plot point list will be extensive. A simple story such as *Moon Over The Brewery* had a very short plot point list; shows such as *Belmont Avenue Social Club* or *Minor Demons* had lengthy outlines.

While structuring your outline, be aware of what your initiating incident will be. The initiating incident is that one thing that propels your story. *Without an initiating incident you have no play.* Here are some examples:

Macbeth—The prediction of the witches. If they don't plant the seed in Macbeth's brain the rest of the play doesn't happen.

The Front Page—Convict Earl Williams escapes from jail. Without this, reporter Hildy Johnson is out the door and there's no play.

The Sunshine Boys—Ben, nephew of a retired vaudeville comic, announces to his uncle that he's found him a job if he will reteam with his despised partner.

Hamlet—Hamlet's dad shows up in ghost form wanting his kid to get revenge.

A Thousand Clowns—Social service folks tell free spirit Murray Burns he'll lose custody of his nephew unless he finds a job.

The Man Who Came to Dinner—Sheridan Whiteside breaks his hip, forcing him to convalesce in someone else's home.

Glengarry Glen Ross—John, the office manager, announces that the valuable real estate leads are being kept overnight in the office safe.

All of the above initiating incidents are necessary for the story to be told. If Hamlet's dad says, "Forget about it, son. Live and let live," there is no play.

Okay, so you've got your initiating incident and you're ready to do your plot point outline. Question: where should you put it?

The initiating incident can be almost anywhere in your first act. But it should without question be in your first act, or in the first fifteen to twenty pages of your play. Although there is a certain flexibility here, it is important to remember that your initiating incident must occur either in—or in the case of *The Man Who Came to Dinner*, before—the first act. You cannot have the initiating incident pop up in the middle of Act Two.

Perhaps your initiating incident is what drives the rest of the play. That's what happens with *The Front Page*. Act One ends with Earl Williams' escape. Sometimes it happens in the very first scene, like in *Macbeth*. Maybe it happens in the middle of the act like in *The Sunshine Boys*.

While going through some old notebooks I found the plot point outline for *Belmont Avenue Social Club*. Look at the logical order of things. Point A cannot happen before Point B and so on.

Initiating Incident: Councilman Petey dies.

Note: This happens before the play starts.

Act One:

    A. Establish Chickie with camcorder.

Note: This may look like a minor thing but it has its payoff in the final moments of the play.

    B. Doug wants Petey's job.

Note: Here is the character "want" that will drive the play.

    C. Fran tells Doug he's giving the job to Tommy. Doug fights back, saying he's the only person who can win against Wesley, a black challenger.

    D. Fran asks Doug to prepare Tommy for the announcement.

    E. Tommy enters. Fran gives him the news. Establish Tommy's bad stomach.

Note: Again, it is important to establish things that will come up later in the play.

    F. Others leave. Doug attempts to prep Tommy.

    G. Doug finds out about Tommy's past rape accusation.

Note: This marks the end of Act One, since this new knowledge is what propels Act Two.

Act Two:

    A. Doug tries to tell Fran about the rape charge but is rebuffed.

    B. Tommy surprises everyone by being quite good in the mock press conference.

Note: This is an example of Aristotle's "reversal." Tommy was set up earlier as an incompetent drunk.

    C. Tommy's newfound ability rankles Doug.

    D. Doug tells others of rape charge.

    E. Tommy explains the charge and defends his innocence. This leads to a stomach hemorrhage and he is rushed to the hospital.

Note: That's why we set it up in scene E above. You just can't have these things come out of nowhere.

F. Doug cancels the press conference and puts his feet up on the desk in victory.

Act Two, Scene Two:

A. Fran gives Chickie slip of paper. The audience doesn't know what's on it.

B. Doug enters. Fran demands rape evidence. Doug's already destroyed it.

C. Doug threatens to blackmail Fran if he doesn't get Petey's seat. Chickie takes the slip of paper, which contains a phone number and dials. Then Chickie exits to men's room.

D. It's Wesley on the phone. Fran gives him Petey's seat.

E. Doug explodes and, with Fran's goading, drops his liberal pretense and calls Wesley a "nigger."

F. Chickie emerges from the men's room with camcorder. He's gotten Doug's diatribe on tape. Fran now has dirt on Doug.

G. Fran explodes, throwing pool balls at Doug.

Note: This is the highest point of action. The climax. Doug exits, defeated.

Except for a few minor moments, this is a very logical list. You could mix it up, give someone the pieces, and they could pretty much put it back together. Notice it tells us almost nothing about the characters. It doesn't have to. This was just the roadmap I followed to write the play.

Having a plot point outline gives you incredible confidence. Before you even write, "The lights rise . . ." you know where you're going. You don't have to stumble around wondering what happens next.

Notice that I have the two things in there that I want to establish: Chickie's camcorder and Tommy's bad stomach. In the first act, they look like amusing character touches, but then they pay off in the second act. Had Tommy gotten sick without setting it up in the first act the audience would have thought that was pretty darn convenient; just an author needing an excuse to get a character offstage.

When Chickie steps back into the room with the camcorder—something the audience hasn't seen since the very first moment of the play—I would always hear a couple of "ah-hah's" from the audience. Chickie and his toy have come full circle.

A WORD OR TWO FURTHER, FROM
PLAYWRIGHT AND DRAMATURG

Emerging playwrights sometimes ask the valid question: "How long should my play be?"

My response is sometimes, "As long as it needs to be." Another way of framing this is "Your play should be long enough to allow your character to change."

As mentioned earlier, your character has to go through some sort of change. In a well-built play, the change usually occurs near the very end of the story. (This also ties in with the Aristotelian "recognition" mentioned earlier.) Your play should build to the character's change and then end. Anything else feels like confusion and bad playwriting. Recall those plays that you have heard read or seen onstage that seem to have multiple endings. Isn't that frustrating? And confusing? So be sure you have a sense of what "the end" means in the world of your play.

In some plays more than one character can change. In *Mister Roberts*, the authors do something very interesting. They have their main character, Doug Roberts, a naval officer in World War II, achieve his moment of recognition and change without even being on the stage. It comes in the form of a letter from Roberts, read aboard ship by Ensign Pulver.

Now, this moment would be nice, but rather anticlimactic if that was how the play ended. However, as the audience processes this, another letter is read, telling us of Roberts' death. The combination of these two letters causes a change in the character of Pulver. Heretofore a comically coward character Pulver seems to grow and, with newfound courage, throws the tyrannical captain's beloved palm tree overboard and takes charge.

It's a great moment on stage. We see the character change right in front of us and then take a courageous action.

Another example of the two-characters-change-end-the-play occurs in *The Little Foxes*. Evil Regina has vanquished her enemies—including having a helping hand in her husband's death—and although victorious feels the need for human comfort to help get her through the night.

In her first "soft" moment in the entire play, Regina implores her daughter, Alexandra, to stay with her for the night. Alexandra, who has not had the guts to stand up to her mother so far, finds the strength to refuse. And then she flaunts her newfound power with the final taunting line to Regina: "Are you afraid, mother?"

Now just because your character has changed, that doesn't mean you have to slam down the curtain. Sometimes you want to give your audience a few moments to let it sink in. This final moment was called the denouement in the old days. That term has become synonymous with "falling action." In other words, you reach your highest point of action—tossing a palm tree like in *Roberts*; violently throwing pool balls in *Belmont*—and then you take a few moments to wrap things up. *Equus* is another good example: the violently stylistic reenactment of the crime is followed by Dysart's final scene, which is much more sedate.

There are rare times when the character appears to change at the end of the play, but really doesn't. This can work as well so long as the point is just that: this character was not meant to change.

The final moments of *The Front Page* rise to a flurry of activity on stage. Then things calm down for the denouement. Hildy Johnson has gone through his change; he's giving up the newspaper business to get married and settle down. Walter, Hildy's editor who has tried to break up the couple, wishes them the best and gives Hildy his watch as a wedding present. They leave and Walter is alone on stage. We now feel the play is over, but Walter makes a phone call asking the cops to bring back Hildy back because, "The sonuvabitch stole my watch."

This is a case of a character who appears to have changed. When we last see Hildy he has lived up to his promise of embarking on a new life. However, we can't help but to think Walter will get him back, one way or another. And as an audience member, that is how I want it to be.

One of the "thoughts" in my play *Desperate Affection* is that it is folly for a woman to believe she can change a man. In the middle of the second act, it looks as though Richard, a hit man in a career crisis, will finally commit to Maddie, the woman he claims he loves. In the last thirty seconds of the play, however, he reverts back to his old ways and walks out. During the rest of the play Richard and Maddie go through a whole plethora of changes regarding their relationship, but if Richard had acquiesced at the climax it would've ruined what I was trying to say. This is that rare instance where the characters really don't change permanently by the curtain.

ON FINDING A PLOT

Which plot is best for your play? In order to figure that out, we better look at your choices.

Aristotle calls the episodic version the "worst of all plots" and we both would have to agree with him. This is especially true if the plot consists of episodes that do not build on top of each other. The above-mentioned whale play, *Top of the World*, is a good example. The scenes in the second act were merely characters commenting on the problem: a Leno-like comedian, the pope, the president. The episodes themselves could have been taken out and rearranged at random. This is a bad sign. When a group of scenes can be thrown together like that it does not result in a well-built act.

So forget about episodic for the moment. Saroyan pulls it off in *The Time of Your Life*, but that play is a very rare animal. While you may argue with Aristotle, he certainly knew a few things about drama, particularly when we dissect both the simple plot and the complex plot.

The *simple plot* usually consists of one clear-cut story thread. Many of the beginning "family plays" we discussed earlier use the simple plot structure.

Look at *The Glass Menagerie*. This plot can be summed up in a few lines. Tom wants to escape his home, but mother Amanda says you can't leave till you find a suitor for sister, Laura. Tom brings home a "gentleman caller" but it doesn't work out due to his engagement to another woman. Despite this, Tom leaves anyway. End of play.

The simple plot works beautifully in *The Glass Menagerie* because it is meant to be a small incident: a few days in the life of a Depression-era family with one simple conflict/unanswered question: Will Laura finally find happiness with a gentleman caller? It has only four characters and tells its story in a very short time frame. Amanda and Tom have the same agenda, albeit for different reasons. To clutter up Mr. Williams' clean, straightforward structure would be like adding a couple balconies to a Frank Lloyd Wright building because you think it is not complicated enough.

Compare this structure to the *complex plot* and use another Williams play, *A Streetcar Named Desire*, as an example. Now you have a larger cast and four very different characters (Blanche, Stella, Stanley, Mitch), each with his or her own agenda. In order to serve the complexities of each character's "want" Mr. Williams must create a much more complicated plot, interweaving all four stories into one cohesive one. Williams is a master at this, and one of the reasons is this: his characters drive the play.

Obviously, there are variations on the episodic plot, the simple plot, and the complex plot—no play fits neatly into any one category. However, nine times out of ten, those variations are dependent upon another factor—a character, an action—in order to build dramatically. Imagine if Tennessee Williams went with his knee-jerk response and made *A Streetcar Named Desire* a comedy (and do not bring up that episode of "The Simpsons"). Or if *The Odd Couple* were rendered a tragedy. Your plot, your characters, and your tone are all ingredients that must be considered when thinking about how to structure your play.

6

CHAPTER

Exposition

HERE'S A SCENE FROM THAT RARELY PRODUCED PLAY, *All Critics Should Be Taken Out and Shot*:

SUSIE: Tim, what are you doing?

TIM: Oh, hi Sis. Just waiting for the mail. Today I'll find out if I've been accepted at Harvard.

SUSIE: That's right. It's always been your dream to go to Harvard. Like our father.

TIM: That's right—Dad did go to Harvard, didn't he?

SUSIE: Why yes, he did. And you'll make a fine lawyer too.

TIM: Well, actually Susie . . .

> (*He gazes longingly at the surgical equipment and blank prescription pads on the desk.*)

SUSIE: What?

TIM: Oh . . . nothing . . .

SUSIE: Mother would have been so proud.

TIM (*Laughing cynically*): Perhaps.

SUSIE: Oh, but she would. If only she hadn't died in that freakishly odd shampoo incident.

Now you know why it's rarely produced.

Exposition is there to give your audience all the facts it needs to understand the play. It can fall into various categories: plot, relationships, backstory. The more plot driven your play, the more important your exposition.

Let's count the facts we've learned in the above scene:

1. Tim and Susie are siblings. The first giveaway is "Sis," which no one I ever met called his sister. This is used primarily in commercials having something to do with laundry. ("Hey, sis, why are your kids' clothes so filthy?")
2. Tim is trying to get into Harvard.
3. Their father went to Harvard. (This is another dead giveaway that they're siblings, as if "Sis" weren't enough.)
4. Their father was a lawyer.
5. Their mother met with an unfortunate end.

These are the facts. But exposition also deals with inferences. Inferences are those things at which you can make an educated guess by the information hinted at. What are the inferences?

1. This is a wealthy family. Harvard-educated-lawyer-dad and the use of the word "mother," where most of us would say "mom."
2. Tim might be interested in something other than the law. I wonder what that could be?
3. Tim and mother had a strained relationship. We know this from his cryptic "Perhaps" and the cynical laugh.

This all seems incredibly obvious, but one would be surprised by the number of plays that practice these kinds of techniques. Everything your character says, every action your character takes, registers with your audience. It's your job to exploit it.

In real life, when people know each other pretty well, they don't need to take the time to explain past history or emotions. Which brings us to one of the big rules of exposition: *Never have characters tell each other things they already know.* This is something Tim and Susie are guilty of.

The problem with exposition is that it is unnatural except in certain cases:

1. A character is new to the situation. *Long Day's Journey into Night* has a very important scene between a new maid and Mary Tyrone in which she fills in a lot of important info. But *she couldn't do it with her husband or two sons because they already know it.* And as long as we're on O'Neill we can also look at his one-act *Hughie.* It has two strangers. It's okay to do

exposition with strangers. Most conversations with strangers are nothing but exposition. This is a good reason to avoid strangers.

2. Characters who haven't seen each other in a long time are ripe for exposition. Just don't base the whole play around it. In Arthur Miller's play, *All My Sons*, Anne comes to see Chris Keller and his family, something she has not done in three years. There has been a great deal of change in the neighborhood and someone (Sue, who conveniently lives next door) has to fill Anne in. Next-door neighbors are quite useful for exposition.

3. Coming from an event. *Who's Afraid of Virginia Woolf?* is a good example of both this and Example 1. George and Martha return from a faculty party and, like most people returning from an event, rehash it and evaluate it. Then two characters new to the situation (Nick and Bunny) arrive.

How many times have you left a wedding, dinner party, or bar mitzvah and immediately started talking about it? In most cases it happens in the car on the way home. I use a funeral in *Belmont Avenue Social Club*. Fran and Chickie have just left the cemetery and, naturally, talk about it. Situations like this allow the exposition to sound organic, not something tacked on by the playwright.

Exposition used to be considered so important to a play that it had its own act. In the classically structured three-act play, it went like this:

Act One: Exposition

Act Two: Complication

Act Three: Resolution

So back in the old days, they would dedicate an entire first act to getting out the facts. If you don't believe us, check out *The Philadelphia Story* (or any Phillip Barry play), *Dinner at Eight*, *The Man Who Came to Dinner*. One of the typical ways exposition was set up was through the telephone call that would start the play. The butler or maid would answer and tell us all, which is why Thornton Wilder makes fun of it in *The Skin of Our Teeth*.

We don't have the luxury of an entire "exposition act" anymore. Modern three-act plays are almost extinct, so playwrights cannot spend a leisurely forty minutes or so setting things up.

So, how do you get that dreaded exposition out quickly and subtly? The first thing you do, and this is the most important, is to realize *how much information the audience needs to know*.

Think of it this way: Exposition is a lot like your family. It can be a royal pain in the ass, but at the end of the day you usually need it. Also, like family, the less you have, the better.

A great example of *just enough* exposition occurs in *Glengarry Glen Ross*. Mamet gives the character of Shelley a sick daughter in the hospital. Why? It ups the stakes and adds to Shelley's desperation to sell some real estate. We know she's sick, we know she's in the hospital, but we never know what is wrong with her. Why? Because it's not important to the overall story.

In my end-of-the-world play *Early One Evening at the Rainbow Bar & Grille*, I never tell the audience what is causing the apocalypse. Characters speculate, but the question is never answered, because it's not important.

Now, this doesn't mean you start your first draft and say, "This is important, this isn't." In your first draft put it all in. Volansky likes to call it the "vomit draft" and encourages playwrights to include every line, beat, instinct you might have had about the ideas, characters, and actions. Cutting later is easy.

Playwrights immediately think that all exposition must be covered with dialogue. It helps, but it should be your last resort. Before you fall back on dialogue, take a good hard look at the setting, the props, the music, and other environmental factors.

1. It is New Year's Eve.
2. The weather is really bad.
3. George made a fool out of himself at last year's New Year's party.
4. Martha is visiting from Alabama.
5. Martha recently quit smoking. George still does a pack a day.
6. George lives in an apartment on the eighteenth floor.
7. The family who lives above George are all very, very, large.
8. George recently became engaged.

These are the bad ways of revealing exposition through dialogue:

1. "Let's have some fun. It is New Year's Eve, you know."
2. "My, that weather certainly is bad out there."
3. "You're not going to make a jackass out of yourself like you did at last year's New Year's Eve party, are you?"
4. "So, how was your flight from Alabama?"
5. "I admire your ability to quit smoking. I myself still smoke a pack a day."

6. "Wow, you can see everything from your eighteenth-floor window."
7. "You know, the family upstairs is very, very large."
8. "I hear you've become engaged."

With the possible exception of number three, these are all bad. There are a couple of slightly better ways:

1. New Year's Eve? A bunch of ways to do this: Remnants of a party. A television broadcast. Offstage noisemakers and shouts.
2. Bad weather? You could do this visually. We see a storm through the window. Or you could have characters enter dressed for bad weather and soaking wet, but never mention it. Trust me, the audience will figure it out.

Then there is the *really* good way: As a playwright you should always be on the lookout for a reason to put your characters into some sort of dramatic tension. Maybe it's not the major conflict of the play, but you need these along the road to keep the audience's attention. And, in this case, to get out the exposition.

So, let's take facts one, two, and three and put them into the form of an argument. George wants to go to a New Year's Eve party; Martha does not. During the course of their disagreement it could come out quite naturally that it's New Year's Eve.

Now we get into the reasons Martha does not want to go. They have to walk ten blocks and the weather is terrible, Martha argues. And besides, she does not want him to make an ass out of himself as he did last year.

And if you wanted to work in number five, you could have George counter with the argument that Martha is cranky due to not smoking and is afraid, if she goes to a party, that she'll start again.

As we move through the list, one can ask how important is it that the audience know Martha is from Alabama? Does it have to be Alabama or just the generic Southern United States? If the state itself is not important then a southern drawl should take care of that. If not, maybe it's in character for her to wear a University of Alabama sweatshirt. But if you have to work it in specifically, let it sound as natural as possible. If you say something like the bad example above ("How was your flight from Alabama?") it screams exposition.

If Martha tells a tale of her terrible flight because there are no direct flights from Alabama to any place on the planet, then at least it sounds quirkier and more natural.

In the case of the cigarettes, you can rely on props to tell the audience the information they need to know: cigarettes, ash trays, matches. The situation between smoker and non-smoker is also filled with dramatic potential.

Do we need to know "eighteenth floor" specifically or just that George lives really high up? If it's the latter, you can do it with the set. If the former, someone could open the door and we see the number 1802.

The very, very large family upstairs sounds as though it has potential to be a running gag. Plaster dropping from the ceiling? Getting stuck in the elevator with them and discussing it as George and Martha enter?

Emerging playwrights try to solve the engagement question by simply putting a ring on Martha's finger, but I might argue that there are several, more effective ways of telling us this information. For example, what is George's reaction to this news? Does the ring become a bone of contention? Does Martha try to keep showing it off and George keep ignoring it? In giving the audience the needed exposition, we also have the opportunity to learn about the characters and their shared history.

Remember: While props and costumes can be a good way of letting the audience in on something you have to make sure that they can actually see what it is you need them to see. A student once handed me a play where a scene ended with the reveal of a character's tattoo. It wasn't just any old tattoo, though. This one had things written on the design that was supposed to tell us a major plot point. Intricate tattoos are difficult to see past the second row, so unless this play was to be performed in the author's garage for her immediate family, this expositional tattoo was a really bad idea.

Volansky's example: I was sitting in the audience of Tom Stoppard's *Arcadia* at the Goodman Theatre in Chicago and, late in the play, my program slipped to the floor. I leaned over to pick it up and missed the four lines of dialogue that explained the relationship between the nineteenth and twentieth centuries—essentially the "ah-ha" moment in the play. I later told Stoppard of this and asked him to please make his exposition a bit longer. The lesson: in addition to making your play director-proof, one should also attempt to make it audience-proof. Or, make sure you have integrated exposition and plot points into the very fabric of your play.

EXPOSITION EXERCISES

Okay, now that you've got one under your belt, try writing a scene that incorporates all these:

Exercise 1

1. X lives in a mobile home.
2. X and Y are sisters-in-law.
3. Y hates mayonnaise.
4. X occasionally shoplifts.
5. X often fights with her neighbor Mildred. Explain why.
6. Mildred is very thin and has strong religious beliefs.
7. Y's husband, Sam, just bought a brand new pickup truck.
8. X has run up some big credit card bills at Wal-Mart.

Exercise 2

1. Today is X's birthday.
2. Y gets annoyed because X spends endless hours on the internet.
3. X used to be a very good tennis player.
4. Y has a puppy that is not quite housebroken.
5. X and Y have very different taste in music.
6. X's brother, Norm, is always mooching food and borrowing money.
7. Y has an addiction to Chinese food.
8. X is an insomniac.

Exercise 3

1. X loves to fish.
2. X and Y have known each other since kindergarten.
3. Y once put X (accidentally) in the hospital.
4. X is trying to sell his boat.
5. Y is college educated; X is not.
6. X can't stand Y's "significant other."
7. X's favorite movie of all time is *Apocalypse Now*.
8. Y has three kids.

Exercise 4

1. X is allergic to cats.
2. X and Y haven't seen each other in fourteen years.
3. Y hates X's choice of clothes.

4. X has an extensive tropical fish collection.
5. Y makes the best grilled cheese sandwiches in the world.
6. Y has a cat named Pooky; X has a dog named Alex.
7. Halloween is the following evening.
8. X has recently been to London.

To accomplish this exercise most effectively, you should start by finding the fact that leads to conflict. We contend that conflict usually stems from something negative, so let us examine those first.

Exercise 1: Y hates mayonnaise. That is certainly negative, but to build an entire scene around it might be difficult. Try numbers 4, 5, or 8.

Exercise 2: Here, 2, 5, or 6 could be possible. One of us would use number 4 in a nontasteful way.

Exercise 3: Number 3 or 6 might be fodder for conflict.

Exercise 4: A combination of 1 and 6 could work. Number 2 might be interesting if the exposition explained *why* they hadn't seen each other in 14 years.

As you look at ways of integrating exposition into your plays, it is important to keep in mind the big picture (remember the outline?) and the following questions:

1. Is the information from this moment/scene/act necessary for the next moment/scene/act?
2. Are you certain that the balance between what the audience knows and what the characters know is correct?
3. Does your exposition follow the rest of the play's logic?
4. Can you faithfully track the exposition throughout the entire play?

A very easy way to ruin your play is through awkward or obvious exposition. You might have the most original idea with the most complicated of characters, but if there is any sense of labored information, an audience will grow bored. A final way to assess the success or failure of your integration of exposition into the fabric of your play is to watch an audience—if they are two steps ahead of the characters, start making some cuts.

7

CHAPTER

Rhythms

SOMETIMES I CAN LOOK AT A COUPLE PAGES OF A PLAY AND, WITHOUT actually reading it, tell the author there's a rhythm problem. How can I tell that? Easy. All the lines look to be about the same length.

How shallow, you gasp. Perhaps. But most times it's the truth. Look below at the scene between Joe and Sally. Since the dialogue itself is not important I haven't written any.

JOE: Xxxxxxxxx xxx xxxxx xx. X xx xxxx x xxxxx xxx. X xx xxxxx x xxxx xx x xxx. Xx xxx xx xxxxxxxx xxx xxx x xxx.

SALLY: Xxxxx x xxx xxx xx x xxxx xxxxx xxx. Xxxxxxxx, xx xxxxx x xxxx x xx x xxxxxxxx. Xxxxxx, x xxx, xxxxxxx x xxxx.

JOE: Xxxxxxxxx xxx xxxxx xx. X xx xxxx x xxxxx xxx. X xx xxxxx x xxxx xx x xxx. Xx xxx xx xxxxxxxx xxx xxx x xxx.

SALLY: Xxxxx x xxx xxx xx x xxxx xxxxx xxx. Xxxxxxxx, xx xxxxx x xxxx x xx x xxxxxxxx. Xxxxxx, x xxx, xxxxxxx x xxxx.

JOE: Xxxxxxxxx xxx xxxxx xx. X xx xxxx x xxxxx xxx. X xx xxxxx x xxxx xx x xxx. Xx xxx xx xxxxxxxx xxx xxx x xxx.

SALLY: Xxxxx x xxx xxx xx x xxxx xxxxx xxx. Xxxxxxxx, xx xxxxx x xxxx x xx x xxxxxxxx. Xxxxxx, x xxx, xxxxxxx x xxxx.

Now, for twelve more pages I see almost *exactly the same amount* of words per sentence. Guess what? That probably means you have a rhythm problem.

Don't think of your dialogue as words for a moment. Think about it as notes of music and all the things that come along with that: tempos, crescendos, beats, fortissimo. Composers are lucky; they get to put all these things into a composition so performers have an idea of how they are supposed to perform it.

A really good, complicated, multilayered piece of music has a little bit of everything in it. It rises and falls. Goes fast and slow. As an audience member, it is far more exciting—and revealing—when you don't know what is going to happen next. When a character that has had logorrhea throughout the entire play falls silent, or utters only one word, we take note. Similarly, think of the number of times you've seen a bad production of a Shakespeare or Restoration comedy. Chances are high that the actors are not following the rhythms that the playwrights put into the text. It is your task to make sure that your characters don't all sound the same.

Playwrights don't have the luxury composers do. Of course, you can rely on stage directions if you must ("This scene should be played at a brisk pace.") but that can be dangerous. For one thing, I know for a fact that directors and actors often dismiss these kinds of suggestions. It is also a bit of a cop-out. Recall what has been said about director-proofing. Finally, what if you the playwright have not given them a reason to play it at a brisk pace. For that to work, there must be an energy, or urgency, within the scene. Otherwise, why play it fast?

However, as a playwright you can get them to at least come close to what you want by thinking of the scene in musical terms. Where do you want it fast, where do you want it slow? Where do you want it quiet, where loud? That's the first thing you have to discover.

It's also important to realize that action can also be used to establish rhythms. In the laconic Cholly and Chickie exchanges in *Belmont Avenue Social Club*, I have them shooting pool. Each performance, the rhythms changed just a beat in accordance to how the game was going. I like to think I was smart enough not to put in the stage directions any details about this. I just say "play pool" and let the scene go from there. These scenes were meant to have a loose, comfortable quality to them. For those of you who have had a pool cue in your hand, you know that this comes rather naturally during a game.

An abrupt action can also change the rhythm. In Arthur Miller's *A View from the Bridge* a playful scene between Catherine and Rodolfo suddenly turns dangerous when Eddie grabs the young man and plants a violent kiss on him.

The previous rhythms now take on a whole new tempo. What was fun and lyrical is now dangerous through the action.

One of my favorite examples of how action and rhythm can be effectively linked is in Wallace Shawn's play *Aunt Dan and Lemon*. The play is set up as a conversation between a sick little girl and the audience, but it soon takes a horrific detour when we discover that the true topic at hand is her beloved Aunt Dan's affection for the Nazis. The childlike words and intonations that begin the play are slowly replaced by the vernacular of the Third Reich.

Varying rhythms becomes especially important in lengthy scenes. If the rhythms are all the same it's like waves hitting the beach. Relaxing, but eventually you'll be lulling the audience to sleep. Remember iambic pentameter? daDUM, daDUM, daDUM. Used alone, Shakespeare's audiences—and generations of tortured schoolchildren—would have been asleep in five minutes. His ability to mix it up with some blank verse, some stressed end syllables, and some trochees make his work transcend simple children's poetry.

Now, don't feel you should change rhythms just for the sake of waking up the customers. *The emotional needs of the scene should determine the rhythms.*

SOME DRAMATURGICAL THOUGHTS

Rhythms in a character can fall into two categories:

1. Interior rhythms—This is the rhythm within a character's dialogue. Is he a slick, fast-talking Harold Hill or a vacillating, unsure Willy Loman? A terse Hedda Gabler or a verbose and self-pitying Uncle Vanya?
2. Exterior rhythms—These are the rhythms characters use in dealing with other characters. They differ from the interior rhythms since they are constantly changing, influenced by outside stimuli.

Look at your own exterior rhythms and voice. You speak one way to your parents and another to your friends. You speak very differently to someone you're romantically involved with than you would with a cop who has pulled you over on the side of the road.

If you have ever had any musical training, some of the terms that we'll be using might sound familiar. Because music is such an important part of Bruce's writing process (and my life), it seemed obvious to us to utilize some of those great Italian words that help convey mood, style, tone, and tempo.

BACK TO BRUCE

Below is a scene from *Coyote on a Fence*, which was rewritten at least a dozen times for rhythm purposes. The content of the scene itself never changed. What changed were the beats within and between the lines.

It was incredibly important to me to vary the rhythms in this scene for a number of reasons:

1. Emotional needs within the scene. This is the next-to-last Bobby/John scene in the play and ends with the news that Bobby has received his date of execution. Bobby stays on a reasonably even keel emotionally within the scene, but John is asked to be: angry, forgiving, momentarily happy/relieved, sorrowful, surprised, frustrated, very angry, and ultimately joyful. That's a lot to ask of an actor in a short scene. If the rhythms are wrong you are making it even rougher on him.
2. The limitations of the actual staging. The scene consists of two men in tiny cells. It's not as if I can suggest staggering amounts of action to back up the emotions. Not much in the way of spectacle to help the emotional leaps and bounds the scene calls for. Therefore it has to be in the words and rhythms.

The scene takes place on Christmas Eve. John has just received an unpleasant Christmas card from a daughter he has not seen in years and starts the scene in a very bad mood.

JOHN: She's nineteen, pregnant, works in a mall in New Mexico and doesn't want me to try and contact her anymore. Her spelling is juvenile and syntax atrocious. Takes after her mother. A fucking grandfather. Jesus . . .

(*Bobby is quiet for a moment, then decides to cheer John up.*)

BOBBY: Dashing through the snow, in a one-horse open sleigh, o'er the fields we go, laughing all the way—ha, ha, ha. Da, da, da-da-da, da da da da da—

JOHN: "Bells on bob-tail ring making spirits bright!" Jesus-fucking-Christ learn the words, will you?

Note: We start with a little sorrow (addolorato) on John's part, then silence, then swing abruptly into a Christmas carol (festivo). This brings a loud explosion from John (fortissimo). In three lines you have three very different rhythms.

BOBBY: Just forget 'em sometimes—

JOHN: Well it's really annoying.

BOBBY: Sorry, I just . . . forget.

(John returns to his mail.)

Note: In the next lines I change the subject to slow down the rhythm (adagio). That's why I want to go out of the last snippet on a tense scene that calls for silence and allows the actor playing Bobby to make the change.

BOBBY: John? We get turkey tomorrow?

JOHN: You new here?

BOBBY: Ain't been outta' lock-up for Christmas. They give us somethin'—don't know what it was—had fat all over it. Weren't no turkey I ever seen. (Pointing to the offstage television) First Christmas tree I seen. Ain't heard a Christmas carol in . . . probably why I forgot. Do they give us turkey, John?

Note: Now it's time for John to change tone. In order to motivate it, and slow down the scene a little, I give Bobby a sympathetic moment. Notice that the dialogue is in a bigger "chunk" as opposed to the tense scene that precedes it.

(John grabs a pen and begins to scribble on one of his cards.)

JOHN: Well, sort of like turkey. Turkey loaf or something. (He hands the card through the bars) Here. It's used. Best I could do.

(Bobby takes the card, looks at it, and then—like a hungry animal—scurries back to his bunk to read it.)

BOBBY: "Wishing you a . . ."

JOHN: "Joyous."

BOBBY: "Joyous Christmas." "Wishing you a joyous Christmas." Man-oh-man, that is so pretty. Snow and all. Can I keep it?

Note: John now takes on a more gentle tone (tenderamente) for the next few lines.

JOHN: Yeah, sure.

(Bobby puts it in a place of honor, then grabs a pencil and begins to scrawl on the back of an official-looking letter.)

BOBBY: Best Christmas I've had in a while, tell ya that.

JOHN: Be a shame if it was your last, wouldn't it?

BOBBY: Ain't gonna be.

Note: A quick rise of excitement in John (giubilante).

JOHN (Moving to the bars, excited): You're kidding!

BOBBY: They got Christmas in heaven too, John.

> (*John processes this and sighs.*)

I'll be right there with Jesus himself.

JOHN: Tell him "happy birthday" for me.

Note: The excitement quickly fades (decrescendo).

> (*Bobby hands the letter through the bars.*)

BOBBY: Here. No picture or nothin'.

JOHN: Thanks. (*Reading it*) Two "r's" in "merry."

BOBBY: You sure?

> (*John looks at the back of the letter.*)

JOHN: What is this? What'd you write on?

BOBBY: Witness thing. They let you bring in two witnesses if ya want but I can't think of no one. You ain't allowed to go—I asked—

JOHN: Oh, like I'd want to—

BOBBY: Couldn't think of nobody else—

Note: This portion should rise to a loud climax (crescendo).

JOHN: When'd you get this?

BOBBY: This afternoon. Chaplain came by and—

JOHN: Today? That sonuvabitch gave you this on Christmas Eve?

BOBBY: Came by to say "Merry Christmsas" and—

JOHN: He is greasing the wheels.

BOBBY: Why would he?

JOHN: Bobby, when they kill you he's a goddamn celebrity for a night! He's on television! People pay attention to him—

BOBBY: Man of God—

 JOHN: Who doesn't give a shit about you or anybody else!

Note: This is the loudest moment in the scene (fortissimo) which now goes suddenly quiet.

> (*Bobby says nothing, then turns to his bunk and pulls out a small package from under the mattress and returns to the bars, handing it to John.*)

BOBBY: Present.

> (*John opens it, then his face brightens as he sees a typewriter ribbon.*)

Note: Suddenly lively and happy (agilmente).

JOHN: I don't believe it, Bobby. Thank you.

BOBBY: Merry Christmas.

JOHN: It's the right one! Ahh . . . this is great! No more carbon paper! Unbelieveable! The New York Times couldn't get me one of these—how'd you manage it, Bobby? Where'd you get it?

BOBBY: (Quietly): The chaplain . . .

　　　(*Lights fade on them . . .*)

And the scene ends on a quiet note.

The reason I use the above scene is because I have seen this play done countless times, from community theatre to London's West End, and it always plays exactly the way I originally wanted it to.

There's nothing mystical to this. It was not hyperbole above when I said I rewrote it twelve times. If anything I underestimated the number of rewrites. I just knew that at this point in the play I needed as many textures as I could think of simply because I was reaching the climax.

What follows this scene is a monologue, which—just by the fact it's a monologue—slows things down a bit. Then I go into the final Bobby/John scene, which has to top the previous one in intensity.

A musical score also has the luxury of accents and various other markings to indicate how it should be played. The playwright has these things too; it's called punctuation.

The biggest mistake beginning playwrights make is overusing the exclamation point. Many feel adding that automatically makes the scene "dramatic." Not necessarily. It just makes it loud. There are those who feel (Volansky) that one is given five exclamation points at birth and one should use them wisely. And probably never in a play script.

The dash (—) and ellipsis (. . .) are both very important. The dash means an abrupt change or interruption. I use it to show a clipped form of dialogue, wherein characters are cutting each other off. I also use it within a sentence when I want something more precise than a comma. ("So I said to Joey—hand me that ash tray, will ya?—that he better get out of here.")

A DRAMATURGICAL INTERJECTION

The ellipsis means a voice trails off, as if the character is deep in thought or cannot finish what he is saying. There was one playwright who came up with a four-dot ellipsis. When someone thought this was a typo she insisted she wanted that extra dot in there. And she expected the actor to perform it. We'll talk about trusting your other collaborators in a later chapter, but suffice to say, they don't want everything spelled out for them.

Sometimes you want a question spoken as a statement. If so, use a period instead of a question mark.

One of the most important things a playwright can do in terms of punctuation is to be clear about how and when each mark is used. While Bruce Graham may have the above rules for what an ellipsis and a dash mean in *his* plays, there are many other playwrights who articulate different rules. For example, I spent the better part of two years telling three sets of actors how to interpret the punctuation in David Mamet's *Oleanna*. Punctuation, like character word choices or actions, should be consistent throughout—I like to call it the "rules of the world." What are a character's daily behaviors? What are the behaviors the same character might display, if pushed to the wall? For you, the playwright, defining these things is part of your job.

Overlapping, or dual dialogue is also a great way establish rhythms. Mamet is great at this. So are Hecht and MacArthur in *The Front Page*. Robert Altman films such as M*A*S*H, *Nashville*, and *The Long Good-bye* use this technique effectively. This form is especially effective to give the audience a feeling of excitement or confusion. It can also be used to reveal aspects of character—don't you know people who constantly talk over others? What does that tell you about them?

BACK TO BRUCE

In my newest play, *Dex and Julie Sittin' in a Tree*, I use it a few times to try and build Dex's frustration. He's trying to talk about something serious but Julie ignores him and buries her head in the refrigerator.

JULIE: I've got gouda, smoked gouda, muenster, cheddar, Monterey Jack, Swiss, Velveeta—which is more of a cheese "product"—

DEX: I keep thinking maybe . . . maybe it can help me figure things out and —why are you doing this? Who cares about the—I'm trying to—

DEX: Fuck the cheese!

Notice there is nothing important to the plot here. If you use dual dialogue make sure it's stuff the audience can afford to lose simply because there's too much going on to expect clarity.

AN EXERCISE

Find a very small conflict between two characters: what television show to watch, what to have for dinner, something mundane. Now, write a fifty-line scene using the following rules:

Lines 1–20: 2–4 words
Lines 21–30: 1–2 words
Lines 31–36: 1 word
Lines 37–38: 35 (or more) words
Lines 39–45: 4–6 words
Lines 46–50: 1–2 words

Don't worry about the scene having a proper ending. Just cut it off when you reach line fifty. What you should end up with is a scene that goes starts off moderately, gets faster, even faster, then slows down, then faster, and even faster again.

You can also adjust the rhythm of a play through the use of monologues. There's something about a monologue that just lets you go nuts exploring a character. You're not worried about the dynamics of other characters interrupting; it's just you and your character.

This all sounds great, of course, until you realize there is one dynamic you have to worry about: the audience.

A DRAMATURGICAL INTERJECTION

One of the mistakes new playwrights make is to assume the audience will be fascinated with everything your character has to say. Having this attitude can lead to deadly monologues.

A deadly monologue is dangerous to the well-being of your story because a monologue momentarily *stops the play*. Drama is based on interaction and the monologue stifles that. Things tend to screech to a halt as your character speaks. Therefore, what they say had best be important.

You should approach a monologue the way you do a play, by asking certain questions:

1. *Will it keep the audience's attention?* This question is harder to answer than it looks for the simple reason you have no idea—until you see it with people in the seats—if it does. Therefore, it's important that you have some sort of "hook" early in the process. The hook is that tantalizing line of dialogue, the unanswered question, that makes the audience want to know what happens next.

2. *Is it absolutely necessary?* You don't want to stop the action of your play for no good reason. Is this monologue essential to moving either the plot or character forward? If the answer is no, cut it.

3. *Does it build? Does it have a beginning, middle, and end?* Look at what O'Neill does in *Long Day's Journey into Night*. The play is replete with monologues and they are very well built. In Act Two, Scene One, Mary begins a short monologue with, "It was my fault." This is a great hook. What was her fault? She then proceeds to list the reasons for her guilt, ending the monologue with, "I never should have borne Edmund." That's pretty dramatic stuff: a mother admitting she shouldn't have given birth to her child. You can't top a moment like that so don't try. O'Neill has reached the emotional climax of her story and wisely ends it.

4. *What note does it go out on? Does it fit in—or fight against—the next moment in the play?* This question relates to the question above. Remember, for the length of your monologue your audience has been—hopefully—listening in earnest. When it ends, their focus will change. Does it shift into another scene or does a character react to the end note of the monologue? A sudden shift of focus is a tricky thing.

Monologues are often related to memories. This is very dangerous territory since memories tend to be "inactive" and you should always be thinking "active." Still, there's nothing wrong with a memory monologue as long as it has some sort of hook and enough quirky detail to make it sound real.

BACK TO BRUCE

In *Dex and Julie Sittin' in a Tree*, I have quite a few memory monologues and to be quite honest, it makes be a bit nervous. Julie's monologue below happens near the end of the play. It's one of those "new information that will hopefully explain everything" monologues.

DEX: So . . . what did you do?

JULIE: What do you think? April 3 I took the first bus to Pittsburgh.

Note: This is my attempt at a hook.

Forgot to take a book, so I read a newspaper I found on the seat over and over. Go ahead—ask me what happened on April 2. John Anderson's pondering a third party candidacy. The prime rate jumped to over 20 percent. Carter urges restraint with Iran.

Note: Why this diversion? Simple—it holds off giving away the hook for a moment. Very rarely in real life to we speak in a straightforward manner, particularly in moments of tension.

(*She looks to him for a reaction; nothing*) Little clinic in a strip mall—very clean—all women. They were in the process of taking down the Valentine's Day decorations and putting up Easter ones, so for a while Cupid was aiming at the Easter Bunny, which was a little disconcerting.

Note: Another diversion. Remember, you always have to know the when and where of what your characters are talking about. Since the timing of this story was important, this was a quirky way of establishing it.

Only takes a few minutes. Hundred and thirty dollars. Cold day for April. I came out and there was a movie theatre across the street so I went in—didn't like coming back here right away. Sat through *All That Jazz* till they got to the open heart surgery and I walked out into the next theater. *Little Darlings.* Tatum O'Neill and Kristy McNicol trying to lose their virginity at summer camp. Bad choice. So I just sort of floated from theatre to theatre. *Kramer vs. Kramer . . . American Gigolo . . . Lady and the Tramp.* I stayed in there till the last bus back. Never took my coat off the whole time.

Note: Again, pay attention to detail. I fixed a date in my head, went to the library, and looked up what movies were playing back then.

Couple days later your letter came back. That's when I cried. For about three days. (*Silence*) If you had just . . . answered the phone.

Note: Now we change tones. It goes from mournful to angry. Without making your character look like a multiple personality, try to get as many emotional textures as you can into a monologue.

Even if you said, "Don't call again" and slammed it down at least I'd know I wasn't . . . invisible. But you couldn't even acknowledge I existed. "No longer at this address." (*Pointing to her head*) Up here, she was always a girl. I almost told you on the phone the other night but . . . that wouldn't work. You had to be here. And I had to tell you because . . . I never told anybody. Not even Steven . . . (*Looking directly at him*) But you were gonna' know tonight. (*She shrugs*) Good for the soul.

>   (*Silence. Finally, she laughs sadly.*)

Well, I got this out of my system. Life goes on. Onward and upward. Once more into the breech dear friends. Know any other applicable cliches?

(*Silence. Dex looks as if he'd like to say something but doesn't.*)

The final reminder about rhythms in a play is that they should be connected to either a character or to a situation. If your character sounds erratic and that is not what you intended, chances are high that it is due to unharnessed rhythms. Pay attention to what a character is wanting to say—and how they are wanting to say it. Without such internal logic, your play will lose its power.

$$8$$

CHAPTER

Troubleshooting from the Back Row

THE FOLLOWING ARE, IN ABSOLUTELY NO RATIONAL ORDER, SOME OB-servations we've both had over the years. Little things that add up that might help your play.

USING PROFANITY

I'm no prude when it comes to language. Sit next to me during an Eagles game sometime and I'll prove it. However, profanity (like all words) is a playwright's tool and has to be used carefully to get the full effect.

Using—or not using—profanity tells us tons about your character and is a very important part of the character voice. It can illuminate all sorts of things about the character. It can tell us about his relation to other characters; does he use it with the "boys" but not in front of women and children? Does he use it out of frustration or an inability to express ideas any other way?

In *Burkie*, Jon pretty much avoids using much profanity. An occasional "hell" or "damn" but that's about it. Then, towards the end of the first act when he and Jess go at each other angrily he explodes, "You're two thousand miles away in the middle of the fuckin' desert, I'm here!"

I remember happily watching the audience do a little double-take at this. Whoa, Jon is mad. If he'd dropped the f-bomb all through the play, however, the scene would have had little impact.

Once again, look to real life. Perhaps you have a friend with a vocabulary like Mary Poppins, but if that friend did come out with an expletive you would definitely remember it.

On the opposite side of the fence is the character for whom excessive profanity is a way of life. Mamet is often taken to task for this, but he's not doing it for a dirty giggle. His characters talk like this and to do it any other way would be dishonest. But even his characters can watch their language when they have to. In *Glengarry Glen Ross* the salesmen speak one way amongst themselves, but take on a very different vocabulary when dealing with a potential customer.

Again, the voice will change with the situation. I do something similar in *Minor Demons*. The scenes between Deke and Vince, two very close friends, are profanity laced. When they deal with other characters, the language changes.

Profanity also comes into play when thinking about the tone of your play. Edgier work calls for edgier language; softer works just the opposite. Listen to the play to see what kind of language the play wants.

I believe *Moon Over The Brewery* has only one instance of profanity. Again, like *Burkie*, it comes at the end of the first act when emotions are hot and Miriam uses "Goddamnit!"

But that's it. Why? Two reasons:

1. I wanted a very sweet tone to what is essentially a very sweet story. Loading it up with profanity wouldn't let me achieve that.
2. The characters just didn't speak this way.

The Champagne Charlie Stakes is another example. This is a love story between two eighty-year-old characters. Profanity would not fit the tone or the character. Again, though, I use one instance of it to show Charlie's anger and frustration as he watches the horse he bet on lose the race:

CHARLIE: Come on you sonuvagun . . . now's your chance—move up, move up . . . come on, come on, come on…come on, come on, come on, come on, come on, come on . . . (*His voice fades as the race ends*) SON OF A BITCH! (*The others jump, shocked*) You son of a bitch, you dirty bastard you . . . you goddamned . . . bastard-son-of-a-bitch…you . . .

> (*The others say nothing, unsure what to do. Then Charlie looks out at the track and brightens.*)

Photo! There's a photo—it's not official!

The profanity is used effectively because it hasn't been used throughout the first two thirds of the play. And I wrote Charlie's explosion with the thought that this is a man who doesn't even know how to swear. Notice how he stumbles around with the words. It would be out of character for profanity to roll smoothly off his tongue.

The world of *Belmont Avenue Social Club* is much different. It's a male-dominated back room of a bar where anything goes language-wise. However, even here I have to pick and choose the profanity. For someone like Cholly it's every other word; for Tommy it's a rare occasion; for Fran it's used for effect.

So be goddamned careful where you use profanity.

PRACTICING WITH ONE-ACTS

For some reason the one-act play has become a vanishing art. There are hundreds of "Ten-Minute Play" contests around, which we find kind of insulting. Why tell an author how long the play has to be? Even more ridiculous is the "Two-Minute Play" phenomenon. Isn't the attention span of the average American audience member short enough already?

Now, if the story you want to tell works out to ten minutes, great. If it works out to two minutes—well, that sounds more like a monologue than a play.

One-acts are a great way to lead up to the full-length play. You can concentrate on a much smaller scale without worrying about plot, structure, conflict. It's like comparing a novel to a short story. A novel needs to follow a longer and much more complicated road. A short story can focus on a smaller incident and luxuriate in detail.

We both encourage students to write one-acts as a warm-up. For one thing, it's not as daunting as attempting the full-length play. You have the freedom to dwell on, say, a specific character you find fascinating without having to worry about all those other things.

As I mentioned earlier, *Burkie* had a warm-up as a one-act. Williams wrote a short play using a Blanche DuBois clone in *Portrait of a Madonna* before attempting *Streetcar*.

The secret to writing a one-act is to think small. This may sound redundant, but beginning writers often feel they have to give an epic feel to what should be minimalist. Keep the number of characters down. Have some sort of dramatic tension or unanswered question, but don't belabor it. Focus on the character. Indulge yourself. Overwrite the first draft (remember that vomit draft?) and then cut.

Looking at the practical side, it is sometimes easier to mount a production of a one-act. Or at least put together a reading in your living room. On the less-than-practical-side, there's no money in one-acts. (Not that there's huge cash in full-lengths. If you're writing plays to make big bucks there's something wrong with you.)

Albee started with one-acts. George Bernard Shaw, Thornton Wilder, Lorraine Hansberry all dabbled in them. Not bad company.

So when the thought of filling up that empty notebook is kind of scary, think about filling up twenty pages of it. Trust me, it's a lot easier.

WALKING THROUGH THE "SET"

The worst thing a playwright can do is sit in his room trying to come up with a play. Ideas don't knock on your door at midnight. (They occasionally call for bail, but that's another story.) As we've said earlier, go out and look for your play. Look for your characters. And once you find them, go and walk through your set.

You've been in your parents' living room a few thousand times. Now you decide to set your play in that room. No problem. You'll do it from memory.

Wrong. You were in that room as a civilian, not a playwright. Go back with an eye and ear for detail. What is it about this room that is unique to your characters? The pictures on the wall? The smell of food coming from the kitchen? The way the sun comes through the window late in the afternoon? Is the television prominent or do bookshelves overshadow it?

In other words, is there anything in your set that tells us about the characters? Is there anything on the set that can shorthand the exposition?

While writing *Burkie* I did just what I'm suggesting you do; I went back and sat in my parents' living room. I noticed a burn hole in a pillow from where my uncle dropped his pipe. That went into the script. Was it a blazingly important ingredient? No. Did people say, "Let's go see that play about the burnt pillow?" God, I hope not. It was just a detail to make us feel we were actually in someone's home and not a set.

Another reason to walk through the set is to find out what you can use for dramatic purposes. I knew I wanted an explosion of violence for the climax of *Belmont Avenue Social Club*, but a fistfight was boring. So I went back to the club, realized the potential weapons that come with a pool table, and used that.

While visiting a prison I was taken back by the constant noise. This becomes important in *Coyote on a Fence*.

Two examples from movie scripts I've written might help clarify this. In *Good Citizen* (which never got made) the climax was a chase scene through a woods. Again, as a fisherman I'd been in various forests quite a few times in my life, but I'd never been chased by gun-toting bad guys. Rather than make it up, I went to a local state park and began to run like a madman through the trees.

Roots, holes, rocks, loose dirt—all these things became obstacles. Then I ran into a particularly dense clump of trees, and was hit by a sudden burst of daylight. I had run off the side of a bluff! The Chesapeake Bay awaited me three hundred feet below. I frantically grabbed the closest tree and, for a few precarious seconds, dangled above the beach. This went into the script. Including the "burst of daylight."

A movie that did get made, *Dunston Checks In*, gave me perhaps my most extreme exercise in walking through the set. Because of a change in location we were forced to use a real kitchen and not a set in the final fight scene. This meant we were very limited in what we could do and where we could put the camera. And if that wasn't enough, we were working with an orangutan named Sam who had to perform a lot of the action.

The producers put me in this kitchen with my notebook and asked me to come up with the scene. I looked around at what I had to work with. Heat lamps! Sam can swing from them. Rows of refrigerator doors. We can use them to smack people. Utensils. Can we get a huge whisk and use it in a sword fight? A bucket and mop sat by the door. Wouldn't it be cool if the bad guy got whacked in the face by a wet mop? (Pretty deep stuff, huh?) I never would have thought of any of it had I sat in the trailer trying to come up with stuff.

So, no matter how familiar you think you are with where you decide to set your play, go walk through it one more time. And take your notebook.

THE AUDIENCE

"You're always talking about the audience."

This was pointed out to me by a student one time. Others in the class nodded in agreement. Volansky has, on occasion, referred to me as an "audience whore." Well, yeah, I do talk about that multieyed monster: the folks who paid to get in, the audience. Because without them, we're nothin'. The fact that the student brought the point up concerned me and I went off on one of my rants. Here is the expurgated version:

There is a tendency today to look down at playwrights who take the audience into consideration. There's an elitism that mere entertainment is somehow not enough for that great temple we call the theatre. If that's the case I've got news for you: the theatre would've died out hundreds of years ago.

I don't mean you should start working pie fights into your plays. Don't feel you have to run out and write the next *Star Spangled Girl*. (Please don't. Even Mr. Simon admits he's not crazy about that play.) The best plays come from some inner passion. Just make sure that passion includes some sort of story and characters the audience (there's that word again) wish to follow on the journey you've created for them.

I rarely actually watch my plays once they're up and running. I know what's going on; I've been to rehearsal. I watch the audience. Are they listening intently? Are they reacting the way I want them to? If so, great.

Are they shifting in their seats and looking at their watches? Uh-oh, I've got problems. (This reaction usually occurs somewhere in the second act.)

Critics notwithstanding (and that's one of the nicest things I've ever said about that group) *it is the audience who will tell you what's right and wrong with your play.*

Now, in order to take advantage of this, you have to swallow some of your ego. Here's an example: Years ago, as artistic director of the Philadelphia Festival of New Plays, I went to the O'Neill Center. A good friend of mine was appearing in one of the plays and when I told him I was coming to see it his jaw dropped and he said, "God, no."

I then went up to the director, a very talented man with whom I'd had many phone conversations but never met in person. I introduced myself, we chatted for a few moments, but then his eyes went wide and he asked, "Why are you here?"

When the cast and director react like this, it does not bode well for an evening in the theatre. And boy, were they right.

It was a self-indulgent piece of crap. Actors rolling on the floor screaming in agony for no apparent reason except that the author told them to. And this was in the first five minutes! Where do you go from there?

The playwright was seated close by and so—out of boredom—I decided to watch him and not the play. He was beaming!

In the first twenty minutes people began walking out. I checked on our friend the playwright. He was still beaming! And nodding his head as if in total agreement with every one of his precious words.

I wanted to smack this guy. Wasn't he watching what was really going on? Didn't he see disgruntled audience members walking out of his show mumbling under their breath?

At intermission I hung close to him, eavesdropping as he spoke with friends. "Going great . . . really terrific . . . maybe I can trim a few lines but I think it's in fine shape . . ." I don't know what this guy was on that night, but put me down for a large prescription of it.

By the time Act Two started over two-thirds of the audience had disappeared and this genius still thought he had a good play. (To the credit of the American theatre it—and its happy idiot author—has never been heard from again.) This guy did not give a damn about the audience. He was so full of himself—the ego I mentioned above—that he did not see the flaws and his play was doomed to fail.

George Burns once lamented the death of vaudeville by saying, "Now young comics have no place to go and be lousy." The same can be said for playwrights. The problem with writing plays is that you *have* to make your mistakes in public. That one-liner you thought was so hilarious while sitting at your desk may be met by stony silence. That emotionally charged dramatic scene may get unintentional laughs. You never know until you see it in public. And when you do, don't be like that clown at the O'Neill. Figure out what is wrong and try and fix it. Remember that it is okay to fail—it goes hand-in-hand with that adage about writing and rewriting.

Do not treat the audience as your enemy. Just because they outnumber you doesn't mean they're out to get you. Really listen to them. Volansky actually hangs around in the women's restroom during previews to hear what the audience is saying about the play. And plays have been reworked and adjusted as a result.

NUMBER OF CHARACTERS

Another common question from my students is, "How many characters should I have in my play?"

The answer: how many do you need?

When it comes to number of characters I'm a firm believer in the fewer the better for the simple reason that it's a lot less work. Every character who steps on stage enters with a history and you're the one who has to create that history. For beginning playwrights, creating a really interesting character is a tough enough job. Go easy on yourself. Keep it small and concentrate making those few characters as richly textured and interesting as you possibly can.

When I'm figuring out my plays the question I always ask myself is: do I really need that character? What is the character's purpose for being in this play? You have to have a very important reason for that character to step on stage. If you can't answer that question, cut him.

Burkie has four characters. In the first draft it had five. Sue, a character we now hear about, picked Jess up at the airport and entered with her. After the first reading the producer suggested I cut her. I resisted, until I got home, read the scene, and realized Sue was simply a Greek messenger who came in and spouted exposition.

Sue served no purpose. I took her exposition, gave it to the other characters, and she was gone, never to be heard from again.

On a more practical—some might say "shallow"—note, a small character play stands a better chance of actually getting produced. Gone are the days of Kaufman and Hart who had the luxury of putting thirty characters on stage (many of whom were their unemployed actor friends).

Actors cost money. Especially if you have to feed them. I know of one producer, and I'm sure there are many, who goes right to the character page and does a quick count. Straight play with twelve characters and you can't double any of them up? The script is tossed. Next!

I will add, however, that if your play demands a cast of forty and a Mexican dwarf, then, by all means, write that play. If you are bound and determined to be a playwright, and have plays that must be written, do not, ever, adjust yourself to suit economics. If it is good, someone will produce it.

CASTING

You should always have a physical picture of what your character looks like. This is very important in the writing process. Then, when you start casting, throw the picture out.

Sometimes a particular physical aspect is important to the story. References are made throughout Mark Medoff's *When You Comin' Back, Red Ryder?* about the character of Angel being overweight. Therefore, you must take this into consideration when casting. But just because your boyfriend has brown eyes, do not turn down a really good blue-eyed actor to play the part you based on him.

The important thing is to find the actor who inhabits the qualities you saw in the character. I learned this when casting *Burkie*.

When the characters are based on your family you have a pretty strong mental picture of what they look like, and this actor looked nothing like my father. But the minute he spoke, I knew I had found my Burkie. Every word out his mouth had a blunt honesty. He had a sneaky sense of humor hiding a pent-up anger. He was perfect.

And my instinct was right. The audience loved him. The only bad review he received came from my father: "That guy doesn't look a damn thing like me."

EAVESDROPPING

I mentioned earlier my penchant for listening in on people. One of the first things we make our students do is go out and secretly tape-record a conversation, then transcribe it verbatim. I always get the same reaction when they hand it in; it made sense when I heard it but on paper it's totally confusing.

This is because it's real.

All through school it's beaten into us to write complete noun-verb sentences, but we rarely speak that way. We speak in fragments and run-ons. All those things that got red ink on your English papers.

The important thing about this lesson is to really hear how people talk and then see how it looks on the page. We interrupt. We finish other people's sentences. We let our thoughts trail off. We go off on tangents.

Before you sit down to write your first play, try the above exercise. Just don't get caught.

DOING IT

Writers write. That probably seems pretty basic but you'd be amazed how many writers—especially those just starting out—don't. In fact, they do the worst thing a writer can do: they *talk* about writing.

They'll tell you in great detail all about their next magnum opus; they'll spill forth intimate details of the characters and plot . . . but they never write the damn thing. Over the years I've had numerous people tell me, "I've always wanted to be a writer."

"What do you write?" I ask.

"Oh, I don't write. I just always wanted to be a writer."

Well, I've always wanted to win game seven of the World Series but it ain't gonna happen. You can, however, be a writer if you write.

It's been my experience that the more a writer talks, the less he writes. I very rarely talk about what I'm writing. My wife may know the general topic of what I'm working on, but knows none of the details until I hand her a first act to read. I don't even tell my agent.

Despite what my father and friends may think (they all have "real" jobs) writing can be exhausting work. If you repeatedly tell people your story it's as if you've been at the notebook for hours actually doing it. Does a bus driver sit in the local bar telling the regulars about each corner he passed that day? Focus your energy on getting it onto paper, not impressing your friends.

On the rare occasions I do speak about my work-in-progress I immediately begin finding fault with it. Just verbalizing any aspect of it makes it sound stupid to me. I begin to try and fix things that haven't even been written yet and this is a huge mistake. The empty notebook is a very scary thing to start with and I certainly don't need to add any self-doubt or anxiety before I've actually tried to start filling it up.

Now this doesn't mean you can't solicit help. Should you hit some sort of snag then yes, ask a teacher or another writer you trust. (If you've got a couple hours to kill you can even ask a dramaturg.) But keep the conversation to that specific problem in your script. Don't use it as an excuse to do the one-person version.

And, if the above isn't enough to scare you out of talking about your writing remember one other thing: it's a really boring topic of conversation.

9
CHAPTER
Collaboration

COLLABORATION IS ABOUT GIVE AND TAKE. IT'S A CREATIVE PROCESS with an exchange of ideas. In order to give you a look at the process of collaboration, the two of us sat down for the following discussion.

VOLANSKY: Okay, all plays are a collaboration of artists but in new plays, collaboration is even more important. Let's start with this book and work our way back to your plays, *According to Goldman* and *Dex and Julie Sittin' in a Tree*. First, as a playwright you're more . . . diligent . . . about writing every day. But as the process of writing this book went on, we sort of became one voice. The voices started blending together into a sort of collective "we," which I think is what a good collaboration is.

GRAHAM: At the end of the day, if you're not sure who contributed what, then it's pretty successful.

V: Well, that's how I feel about being a dramaturg. If I'm sitting in the audience on opening night and I can identify the things that "I did" then I know that I've failed in my job. During the collaboration of *According to Goldman*—

G: I'm still not sure who did what.

V: That was a really hard process. Not necessarily for you and me, but there were a lot of brains in the room. There was some tension sometimes. How would you articulate that particular process?

G: You want actors to be comfortable with what you've given them to say. There's nothing worse than watching an actor struggle because you haven't given him enough motivation or the dialogue's awkward. The most common problem I've found is the emotional transition. You don't give them enough beats to make them shift emotionally the way you want them to. For instance, I was in a production one time where my character had to say, basically: "No, I won't do it . . . no Victor, please . . . no, you can't make me! . . . okay, I will." All right, I'm exaggerating, but that's pretty close. You could tell this author had never been on stage in his life. He's asking the actor to make an emotional transition without giving him either the proper motivation or time to do it. That's why it's important for every playwright to spend some time on the boards. It teaches you not to make impossible demands on an actor.

The problems with *Goldman* were with the characters, especially the wife. I wasn't always exactly sure what she was doing—what she was thinking—at all times. How many times did we rewrite her scenes? And I'll rewrite it again with the next production. I made some changes in the opening scene to make an actor happy. I'm going back to the original when I rewrite it. It wasn't awful or anything. I tried it. It didn't work.

The whole process of giving actors new pages is tough. You've got a three-week rehearsal period and they have to digest it and hope it makes some sort of sense. But it's important for playwrights to know that you never give the actors the new pages first.

V: Absolutely. Explain the process.

G: First, we figure out what the problem is. Then I go off and write and give the pages to you. You'd give me a reaction, maybe I'd rewrite or cut, then we show them to the director (Pamela Berlin). We'd get her reaction and the three of us would work together on those pages. Then, and only then, would we give the pages to the actors. I've seen playwrights who give the pages to the actors first. Wrong.

V: That's deadly. Like playwrights who want to give direction.

G: Exactly. If I have a problem with something the actor is doing I always go through the director. Now there have been times when the director has asked me to speak with an actor, but that's different. Now it's a collaboration instead of a mutiny.

V: Part of it is putting on a unified front. For instance, if a playwright has a disagreement with a director, take it out of the rehearsal room and do it in private. Particularly with new work. I think the way we did it—playwright, dramaturg, director—is the best model.

G: Unless one of us is an idiot, yeah.

V: Rule number one: try not to collaborate with idiots. Go back to *Goldman* and the building of that play, especially the wife, Melanie. Looking back, do you feel you missed anything?

G: Yeah, which is why I'm rewriting it. I missed a huge step in the tension of their relationship. You had a married couple who always worked, now they're semi-retired and see each other 24 hours a day. That's a big difference in a relationship. All sorts of tension. You see a lot of divorces of recently retired people because they can't stand being together all the time. And I never acknowledged it.

V: Why did you miss that?

G: I don't know. Busy appeasing actors and dramaturgs.

V: Seriously.

G: I don't know. You have to step back from it before you see things. That's why I don't like to go to rehearsal that much. (Director) Jim Christy says I'm the closest thing to working with a dead playwright. Some playwrights want to be in rehearsal eight hours a day. That's a mistake.

V: I agree.

G: Let the actors and director have some freedom. They become inhibited when the playwright is in the room; they're afraid to question the text and play around with it.

V: That's why mallaturgy is so good.

G: What is that?

V: That's when the dramaturg takes the playwright to the mall or something. Gets him out of the room. Do you think you were too on top of things in *Goldman*?

G: No, I tried to get out of the room. But the play needed work and we were out-of-town, so I had no place else to go but rehearsal. I got away as much as I could. Let them experiment. Try things. Most times I'm pleasantly surprised when I come back. Sure, sometimes you have to say, "No, sorry, doesn't work," but most times it does. I see things I never thought of when I was writing the play. A smart director and cast are always going to find ways to make you look good.

V: *Dex and Julie* is early in the process. You've only heard one reading of it. How do you feel about the foundation of the play at this point in time?

G: Well, one problem is what I mentioned earlier. In the second act I make Dex shift emotions too quickly. I don't give the actor enough beats to make the change believable. I ran through the emotional changes in the writing. Luckily it's a short act so I have the luxury to go back and fix it. I also have to make sure Julie's "want" is clear. And it can always be funnier.

V: You do something I wish more playwrights would do: you lock your friends in your house and read the play out loud with a small audience. You place a lot of importance on having an audience.

G: When there's an audience I pay more attention to the play. My mind doesn't drift. Of course, if my mind drifts too much there's something wrong with the play. But if there's an audience I'm much sharper. I'm watching them and not the play. Hell, I know how the play ends.

V: I imagine you subscribe to the, "go see plays, get to know theatre artists," school of thought.

G: Absolutely.

V: But you hate other playwrights.

G: No I don't. I just hate other people in general. You have to be careful not to insulate yourself with just theatre people. Getting to know people in the business is very important, but you can't lose track of real life. Otherwise, you start writing plays about being in the theatre. Go out to Hollywood and look at a list of new plays opening. They're all about the movie business! Give me a play about real people with real problems, not this microcosm of society.

Seeing plays is absolutely essential. When I was a kid I read every play in the Ridley Library, then got on my bike and read every play in the Swarthmore Library. I ask my students every class, "See any plays this week?" And I might get a hand up once in awhile. There are plays right on campus! "Gee, I might have to cross the street." It's very frustrating. You can't be a playwright and not go see plays.

V: And on the other hand you get the student who lives in the theatre. I sometimes tell my drama students to get out of the theatre and go see a lacrosse game. Go see a lecture on globalization. And they look at me like I've got four heads.

G: Exactly. It's balance.

V: You can't begin to depict how people live unless you're out there observing it.

G: Okay, now: what's your job? How would you describe the duties of being a dramaturg? You know, if you type "dramaturg" or "playwriting" spell-check nails them as nonexistent words. Shows how far up the food chain we are.

V: I'm stalking Bill Gates about that. "Please add us to your dictionary."

I define a dramaturg as someone who advocates for the text. And it takes a myriad of forms, such as making sure the actors know the world in which their character is living, to—in a new play situation—knowing what the playwright's intentions were. Or at least having some sort of understanding of what the playwright is trying to do. I look at the situation and say, "If you're telling me this scene is about 'hope' but I'm seeing 'despair' then we've got a problem here." A dramaturg is really a Monday morning quarterback.

In terms of picking a play—or "responding" to a play is maybe a better way of saying it—it all goes back to the story for me. I like to listen to really good stories. I've dabbled with the avant garde; I love to see experimental work. As long as there's no peanut butter and salami involved. But I feel as human beings, we want to connect to the play. We want someone on stage to identify with. Follow that character's journey. So the plays I respond to have compelling characters in interesting situations.

I try to coach a playwright into being really clear about what the characters' objectives are. The logic behind the characters' action must make sense. We must be clear that we can get from point A to point B to point . . . you know, all those other letters.

G: The logical construction of the character's action. That was one of the problems we had to work on in *Dex and Julie* in the first act. Julie's action made no sense.

V: *Why* a character does *what* a character does *when* the character does it. Does that make sense? Because it's very important.

G: I guess. What do I know?

The rewrite process. It's kind of impossible to write a chapter about how to rewrite because every instance is different. What are the do's and don'ts? What's the worst thing a playwright can do in that situation?

V: Not remembering what the original intent of the play was. I've worked with playwrights who have workshopped their plays in different cities and they've gotten notes, obviously, and they rewrite the play based just upon those notes rather than what the initial impulse behind the play was. The play becomes diluted, diffused—and it's not what the playwright wanted to say in the first place. There's no sense of "self" in the play because the playwright's trying to make everyone happy. If you start rewriting to someone else's vision of your play you're just going to run into problems. You have to be open to notes, but choose the ones that fit what you're trying to say. And it takes experience to know the difference.

G: It does. When I first started out I fought every note.

V: Which is wrong. But at the same time, you can't just roll over and take all of them. There are times when I've heard dramaturgs give notes and I think, "That's not what this play is trying to be."

G: Once I learned to stop fighting with people, I found that I could get hit with a hundred notes. I listen to all of them, then maybe use six. But it didn't cost anything—except a little time—to listen to them.

I've asked everybody this so far: what's your worst experience in working with a playwright?

V: I have been pretty lucky actually. There was one bad experience. The playwright was not around in the early days of rehearsal and I was checking in after every rehearsal with my assessment of the process. And the director was furious because she thought I was spying. So I guess it goes back to the idea that when you start rehearsal it needs to be very clear from the first day what everybody's role is. What are the expectations?

G: And the chain of command.

V: Exactly. Who wants the notes first? With Pam on *Goldman* she trusted us to do the first pass. We brought her more polished pages and saved time. Some directors want to be in the loop immediately. Production's tough enough with a new play—why add to the tension? Start off by getting a clear procedure for the rewrites. Lay out those rules first and you'll save yourself a lot of grief.

I once worked on a play where I was caught in the middle. A playwright with a strong point of view and a director with a strong point of view. And the play needed work. The playwright felt the play was done because she'd seen it a couple places and people said nice things. If anything hurts a playwright in the rewrite process it's an audience fawning over them. And I felt like I was standing in the middle—and I love playwrights and directors!—but it was really hard.

One of the problems was that the playwright had something in her head she wanted to say but it wasn't on the page. And she was adamant that it was in the script. And I kept saying, "Show me *on the page* where it says this." It wasn't there. Just because it's in your skull doesn't mean it's on the page. And that's a common problem for playwrights, don't you think?

G: That's why it's a huge mistake for playwrights to direct their own stuff in early productions. You need a third eye. What was so crystal clear to you while working in the notebook isn't always so clear when you put it on stage.

V: *Dex and Julie* was like that.

G: Oh God, it was mud. I needed the feedback of the actors, director, dramaturg to get me on the path of righteousness.

V: That's one of the big misconceptions about dramaturgs: "I know better than you. I'm here to fix your play." What I do is coaching. Ask the playwright questions. I feel as though some of the best dramaturgs are not aspiring playwrights—it takes away the feeling of competition. I just ask a lot of questions because, frankly, I don't know what it is really like to write a play.

G: Right. If you come at me and ask questions I don't get confrontational. And if I can't answer your question, there's probably a problem with the script.

V: One of the questions I like to ask playwrights is, "What can we do to really screw up your play?" And it's so illuminating what playwrights do not see in the world of their play.

G: That's a tough question to answer.

V: It is. But it's a good question to ask because they really have to think about a lot of different things, both from the script point of view and the production point of view.

Do you read the critics?

G: I did when I was starting out. Not anymore. I leave town after an opening. And it's not just about bad reviews. I've gotten some great reviews that I thought were pretty stupid. If they're hanging in the lobby I read 'em because I'm hanging in the lobby, too. I think beginning playwrights should read them but it is death to take them seriously. They're just one audience member. However, if the audience tends to agree with them en masse, you better listen. Trust me, I'm tougher on my plays than any critics.

V: What do you like in a play?

G: Same thing you do. A story's important, but it's more the characters for me. *Glass Menagerie* has ten minutes' worth of plot but I love being in that cramped apartment with those characters. And I always hope it's going to end differently! I want Laura to get her gentleman caller every time I see it, but it never happens. I want Blanche to run off with Mitch.

V: *Streetcar* is my favorite play, and I think it is in Scene Six that ends with, "God is present so quickly." The lights come down and I think, "This time it's going to be a happy ending." Every single time.

G: The really great plays are the ones where you walk out and say, "Well, I'll see that character tomorrow." They don't go away just because the play is over. They live on after the curtain.

V: Do you know the story about Tennessee Williams laughing uproariously at the end of *Streetcar*? And someone said, "What are you laughing at?" and he said something like, "Oh, that Blanche. She'll be out of that sanitarium in a week on the arm of a doctor."

G: A playwright has to be thinking about what happens to the characters when it's all over. I'm going through that with *Dex and Julie* right now. I can tell you all about what happened to my characters after the lights come down. You have to know that stuff.

V: Do you think television and movies have caused a shift in playwriting? I'm seeing plays that create a world that's difficult to put on stage. It depends too much on visuals—

G: Twenty scenes in the first act. I usually hate plays like that. My plays are pretty much lights up, lights down, intermission. *Early One Evening at the Rainbow Bar & Grille* is totally unity of time, place, and action. One of the great things about theatre, as opposed to movies, is that the lights can come up and we sit there and let the characters wash over us. What playwrights have to remember is that every scene has to go out on some sort of super moment. And when the lights go down you momentarily lose the audience and then have to get them back. I've learned from experience that even with a two-act play you have to do something early in the second act to get the audience back into it. They've been out in the lobby, calling the sitter or getting a drink, and they're not focused on the play right away. The best thing is to put a big laugh in the first two minutes of the second act. That grabs them and they're back into it.

V: I've been advocating the ninety-minute, no intermission play because it's becoming so hard to get the audience back. What do you think about "topical" plays?

G: As long as there's some sort of universality about it, no problem.

V: Like *Angels in America*?

G: Yeah, I guess. The topicality went beyond just AIDS. You can apply that play to a lot of things. The problem with a topical play is that people want to get on their soapbox and forget about the characters.

V: What's the best play you've seen recently?

G: *The Pillowman*.

V: Why do you like it?

G: It hits on so many issues. Personal freedom. How's an artist created? How an artist uses other people. And it was done in a way that unsympathetic characters were sympathetic. The characters all went through a change. I had no idea where it was going; I never got ahead of the playwright. He was always two steps ahead of me. And I laughed like hell. What is yours?

V: You know, I've seen some terrific plays. I loved *The Pillowman* for the reasons you said. I also love McDonagh's *The Lieutenant of Inishmore* because it was constantly surprising me. I love whatever Bruce Norris writes and his plays *The Pain and the Itch* and *The Unmentionables* both entertained me and made me think a great deal.

G: Nice. Should we wrap this up with something clever and pithy?

V: You go type it up. I'll try to think of something.

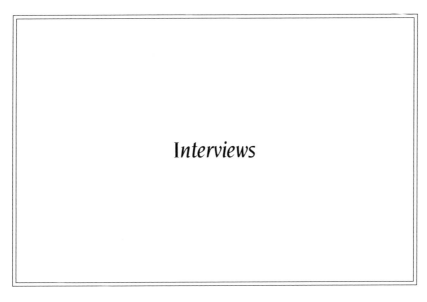

Interviews

WHEN WE STARTED DISCUSSING THE DETAILS OF THIS BOOK, WE KNEW we wanted to talk about theatre—specifically playwriting and collaboration—from several different perspectives. To that end, we both talked to and emailed a wide variety of our colleagues who were at different stages in their theatrical careers. As the theatrical process is generally made up of people from all sorts of different backgrounds and experiences, we wanted to tap into that sense of diversity. We have learned a great deal from the range of responses that we received and hope that you will too.

CAROLINE LUFT

Caroline Luft is a writer and actor based in New York. Her play Goodbye Stranger *was commissioned and premiered by Steppenwolf Theatre Company, directed by Polly Noonan. Her essay about corunning a theater company, "I Didn't Always Think They Were Assholes," was published in the collection* Personals. *She has been a Fellow at the Hawthornden Castle Retreat for Writers in Lasswade, Scotland, and a collection of her short plays for young people,* Cool Guys Don't Go Out with Smart Girls, *is published by Baker's Plays.*

How do you define collaboration?

Any project which involves the efforts of more than one person qualifies as a collaboration—literally "working together." I suppose even projects that happen in separate installments (for instance, translations or adaptations that occur without involving the original creator) would count as collaborations.

How do you measure a "successful" collaboration?

a. A successful collaboration would be one in which the resultant whole is truly greater than the sum of its parts. Each individual's contribution serves to uncover the potential of the whole—sometimes illuminating facets not even anticipated.

b. Any project after which the participants are still talking to each other.

How do you measure an "unsuccessful" collaboration?

a. Frankly, any project that is disappointing to a single one of its contributors could be labeled "unsuccessful." Unfortunately, even with a feel-good hit, somebody's bound to have been disappointed or frustrated along the way. If one removes feelings and ego from the equation, an "unsuccessful" collaboration would be one in which the component parts do not cohere.

b. Someone quits.

What are three things you have learned about the theatre?

"Theatre people" are not, on the whole, noble or special. This realization came as soul-numbing disillusionment, but learning the truth has been helpful.

It is very, very hard to produce a play. At all. Even the crappiest showcase in a leaky blackbox with duct tape holding the curtains together took more effort (and, more often than not, more money) to mount than one would like to imagine.

One should feel free to walk out of bad theatre (waiting for a scene change or an opportunity to slip away unobtrusively, of course). Sitting through too much bad theatre will take years off your life. Even if you've gone to support a friend—you can always hide in the lobby and reappear at the end—and even if the ticket price set you back, it is almost always justifiable to leave. Chances are, the second act will not get better.

What are three things you have learned about playwriting?

There's a reason it's "play-WRIGHT," like "wheelwright," not "play-write." A play needs to be wrung and wrought and wrested into being, forged, mushed, whittled, and burnished. Even while it's still on the page, a play is three-dimensional.

Very smart people can be very bad playwrights. And even good playwrights can write bad plays.

It is better to listen to your characters than to put words in their mouths.

How do you, as a playwright, build relationships with theatres?

From observation* it seems that initiating communication (usually written, then leading to actual phone calls and maybe even coffee or a cocktail) with

---

*My own experience has been much more random. I have relied on coincidence and the recognition of former fellow interns.

the Literary Manager of a given theatre company is the traditional way to start a relationship. Even if the company doesn't select your play for production or development, if the Literary Manager asks for your next script, that's a good sign. Of course, if you never hear from them, or if they won't accept an unsolicited submission, it's impossible to start (let alone build) a relationship, which can be quite frustrating.

Theatrical artistic and administrative staffs tend to have frequent turnovers, which is why it's important to try to stay aware of "who is where." (The Internet can be a great help in perusing staff lists.)

Try not to be the lonely playwright who doesn't know any other writers, let alone actors or directors. Having acquaintances involved in the theatre (especially actors) means that you will more than likely be invited to productions, readings, workshops, and the like. By attending you can get an idea as to whether you are interested in that company's aesthetics, mission, vibe, members, space, etc., and, if so, perhaps even be introduced to a human being who reads scripts for them.

How do you, as a playwright, build relationships with other theatre artists?

I remember everybody. I remember names from one-act plays I saw in a basement ten years ago. And I retain the names of people—performers, writers, directors, designers—I think are good, and make mental notes to try to work with them someday if an opportunity presents itself. I ask friends, "Who was that woman in your ten-minute subway play? Do you think she might be interested in doing my reading? Do you mind if I email her?" More often than not people are flattered to have made an impression, and are excited to be considered for a project. (Sometimes not, of course.)

I think the most important element of a working relationship with another artist—let's say playwright and director, or playwright and dramaturg—is the sharing of a vocabulary. You need to feel that you and your collaborator(s) are speaking not only the same language, but the same shorthand.

What was the most helpful piece of advice you ever received about working in the arts? Who gave it to you?

I hope it's okay to answer this question with quotes that weren't given to me directly, but those which I've found helpful.

"It's called letting go of your illusions, and don't confuse them with dreams"—Stephen Sondheim, "Now You Know," from *Merrily We Roll Along*.

"It is better to destroy than to create that which is inessential"—Federico Fellini, 8½. (For a long time I mistranscribed the quote as "It is better to do nothing than to create that which is inessential," which was a very handy rationalization for procrastination.)

I find the following anecdote illuminating because it's only human that a writer craves feedback, assurance, and a directive from some external source (especially a respected mentor):

> "Then I said, 'You know, I don't know if I want to write anymore.' To make [Robert Penn Warren] really come out and say—who knows, whatever—because he'd already told me, 'No one writes dialogue better than you.' Now, I've interrupted his dinner, he's been very gracious, and I say that, and he looks me in the eye and says, 'Understand, David. I don't give a shit who writes and who doesn't.' In other words: If you, David, are soliciting from me 'Oh, you must,' I ain't gonna say that, because that's up to you."—David Milch (creator of "Deadwood")

What piece of advice would you share with emerging theatre artists?

1. Read as much as you possibly can. Read ravenously—fiction, nonfiction, science, biography, autobiography, poetry, even plays if you feel like it. Read about the lives of writers, whether you know their work or not. Read Malcolm Cowley's *Think Back on Us*, and read the *Paris Review* series of interviews with writers, "Writers at Work."
2. Everything takes much longer than you think it will.

KRIS ELGSTRAND

Kris Elgstrand was born in Vancouver, B.C., but raised in the suburbs. His play The Boys *received its world premier at Azuka Theatre in Philadelphia. His collection of one-acts,* Black Codes: Three Plays, *toured Canadian and U.S. Fringe Festivals in 2001 and was subsequently produced off-off-Broadway. In addition, he has developed work at Canada's prestigious Banff PlayRites Colony.*

His other plays include The Job, Life with a Hole in It, *and* The Ramifications of a Car Crash. *As a screenwriter and producer, Kris' work includes the short film,* Man Feel Pain, *winner of the Bravo FACT Best Short Film Award at the Toronto International Film Festival, 2004. In 2005,* The Cabin Movie, *a feature film Kris wrote and coproduced, received its world premiere at the Toronto International Film Festival and went on to be screened at festivals across the country. It received its U.S. premiere at Methodfest in Los Angeles.*

How do you measure a "successful" collaboration?

I usually consider a collaboration to be successful if it produces a positive result. A positive result could be just about anything good you can take away from the experience whether it's the satisfaction of artistic achievement, the creation or strengthening of a relationship with a fellow artist, or the personal development that comes of tackling something that might seem to exceed one's abilities. Of course, not all these things will reveal themselves as positives when you're in the middle of the collaboration. You might, in fact, want to kill yourself and/or your collaborators at any (or every) point in the process. This doesn't mean the collaboration isn't successful, just that you're collaborating.

Ultimately, the most successful collaborations I've enjoyed have created strong work in an environment in which all the participants are mutually respected, trusted, and relied upon for their individual abilities and strengths. However, that doesn't necessarily mean that it's easy or that you'll still like and respect everyone by the end.

How do you measure an "unsuccessful" collaboration?

On my good days I think there is no such thing as an unsuccessful collaboration. On my bad days, I think all collaborations are doomed to be unsuccessful. The collaborations I would consider to be unsuccessful are those that don't produce an identifiable positive result. Aside from things like laziness and lack of mutual respect, the leading cause of unsuccessful collaborations is ego. A healthy ego is required to create any work of art. Excessive egos, however, generally lead to destruction rather than creation. For whatever reason, if the work is garbage and you had an awful experience creating it, the collaboration was unsuccessful.

What are three things you have learned about the theatre?

1. Though it can be great fun and most rewarding, it's never easy.
2. It's really difficult.
3. No matter how much you do it, it doesn't really get any easier nor does it pay well.

How do you build relationships with theatres?

I don't build relationships with theatres though I recognize the fact that, as a playwright, I really should. Here's what I think I should do:

Go out to see more plays.

Contact and meet the people whose work I've liked or been moved by.

Keep in touch with producers, artistic directors, actors, directors, other playwrights, and members of the theatre community.

Take advantage of any and all opportunities to get my work in front of producers and artistic directors and follow up whenever and wherever possible.

I guess one last option is to be really rich and make large charitable donations.

What was the most helpful piece of advice you ever received about working in the arts? Who gave it to you?

My boss, Martin Kinch (founder of the Toronto Free Theatre) was a student of Marshall McLuhan's at the University of Toronto. Martin told me that Mr. McLuhan had a wonderful sign behind his desk that read, "Artists make art. They don't like art." I always thought that was true and, in a bad way, I feel it's given me license to be bad at many of the things that are so important in the two previous questions.

Some great stuff from David Mamet:

"Nothing replaces the investment of time."

"The process of writing is the process of overcoming the self-loathing attendant on the process of writing."

What piece of advice would you share with emerging theatre artists?

All that Joseph Campbell stuff about following your bliss is actually true. Focus on what you want to do and do it. Other than being exceptionally lucky, that's the only thing you can do.

LAURA EASON

Laura Eason is the author of ten plays. Her work has been commissioned and produced by Lookingglass, Steppenwolf, Sojourn, Walkabout, and Touchstone Theaters as well as Middlesex School. Laura is an ensemble member and the former artistic director of Lookingglass, an associate artist with Sojourn Theatre, and the recipient of an NEA Artistic Development Grant and a "Jeff" for Best New Work. Also an actor, Ms. Eason has performed at BAM, Lincoln Center, and on Broadway in New York and regionally at Berkeley Rep, Seattle Rep, McCarter, Arden, Steppenwolf, Goodman, and in more than twenty shows with Lookingglass.

How do you define collaboration?

Collaboration can really vary depending on who is in the room and what you are working on. But I define collaboration like this—if everybody in the room—no matter what their official job description is—feels comfortable and is welcome to weigh in or give their opinion on any aspect of what anyone else in the room is doing, then it's collaboration. Of course, the opinion giving might exist within certain parameters and the shape of it can take many forms, but if everyone can be a part of the whole picture, then to me it's real collaboration. And, of course, best idea in the room wins.

How do you measure a "successful" collaboration?

In making a new piece with a group of artists—I think collaboration is successful when everyone who has been in the process feels that they were able to be a part of it in the way they wanted to be—that they felt their ideas were heard and seriously considered and they were not asked to worry about or think about things that they didn't care about or weren't interested in.

In two different groups coming together to make something—I think successful collaboration in that situation is when the two groups make something that neither could or would have made on their own that is a combination of what the two different groups do best without one voice dominating the other.

But I must say, I am talking only about process, not about product.

How do you measure an "unsuccessful" collaboration?

Unsuccessful collaboration is when people don't feel heard or feel marginalized in the process—overlooked and/or underappreciated. But this is about process. I have had several "unsuccessful" collaborations that have resulted in a "successful" product.

What are three things you have learned about the theatre?

It is harder than you'd think to make a good play.

Just do it yourself. If no one will produce you, take the power and produce yourself, get some friends together and put up some work — only good things will come of it no matter if the project is outwardly successful or not.

You really do have to do it for the love because along with the deep soul satisfaction comes tons of heartache and disappointment and an even smaller than imagined paycheck, even at the highest levels.

Bonus answer—no matter how successful you are in the theater, people will never stop asking you if you've been on TV.

What are three things you have learned about playwriting?

It is harder than you think to write a good play.

You write how you write. Explore others' approaches and techniques if you want, but follow what works for you. If you're someone who thinks for a long time but doesn't sit at the computer until it's pretty far along in your head, do that. If you are someone who sits at the computer from 6 A.M. to 10 A.M. every day, come hell or high water, great. But neither approach means anything about quality or artistry. You have to have and be true to your own process.

Believe that each project is valuable and feeding into your work and your art even if it doesn't get produced or if people don't understand or like it.

How do you, as a playwright, build relationships with theatres?

Meetings, seeing and supporting theatres' work, relationships with directors are big. I also am part of a company and that has shaped how I build relationships, by bringing artists into my company and developing those relationships outside my company.

How do you, as a playwright, build relationships with other theatre artists?

Gather them together—get some artists over and do a reading and get people interested in your work. Actors are amazingly open to doing readings, I have found. Organize readings with actors and invite directors you know to come and listen and talk about the play. It can be very lonely, and the more you can connect with people, the better. Or form a playwriting group where you meet other writers. Of course, there are a million things—apply to festivals and development situations that are great—but you don't have to rely on anyone else or any organization to make relationships and have things happen. And school helps many people—undergrad and grad school—and can be key in developing your future professional relationships and opportunities.

What was the most helpful piece of advice you ever received about working in the arts? Who gave it to you?

Focus on the art above all—there is a great blessing in getting up every day and being an artist that has nothing to do with money or fame or reviews or who thinks you're cool. My first mentor, Joyce Piven, who runs the Piven Theatre workshop outside Chicago, gave it to me.

What piece of advice would you share with emerging theatre artists?

Basically, the same—if you're in it for the long haul, really figure out what you want to make and make it and don't get too caught up in things outside yourself—reviews, buzz, hype, who else has what—just do your work.

DENNIS REARDON

Dennis J. Reardon's first play, The Happiness Cage, *was produced by Joseph Papp at the Public Theater in 1970. Papp subsequently produced Reardon's* Siamese Connections *and—on Broadway at the Booth Theatre—*The Leaf People, *the epic saga of an Amazonian tribe. Since then, Reardon has won national play awards from the Weissberger Foundation, the National Repertory Theatre Foundation, and Theatre Memphis for his plays* Steeple Jack *and* The Peer Panel, *both of which are published by Broadway Play Publishing along with his most recent plays,* The Misadventures of Cynthia M. *and* Last Days of the High Flier. *He is a recipient of a two-year NEA Playwriting Fellowship. He has served as the head of the Playwriting Program at Indiana University since 1987.*

How do you define collaboration?

More than lip service must be paid to the cliché that "we're all working to serve the text." The partial proof that assertion is to be trusted comes when the director and designers (and producer, if it's a guy like Joe Papp) ask useful preproduction questions of the playwright, which means that they've read the text well enough to be intelligent about it. Once rehearsals begin, the director must ensure that the actors are comfortable in the presence of the playwright and, conversely, that both actors and playwright are "protected" from each other. I truly believe in the director as mediator and buffer. The moment the director violates my trust, the "collaboration" is over and it simply becomes an ugly dogfight to control the text.

How do you measure a successful collaboration?

A collaboration has been successful if, by opening night, I have not killed the director. It is wildly successful if, after the production, I discover that I would like to work with that director again. This has happened exactly once in thirty-six years' worth of productions.

How do you measure an unsuccessful collaboration?

Once, in the greenroom of the Booth Theater during rehearsals for my epic *The Leaf People*, I was ready to physically assault the director. I would have, too, had Joe Papp not interposed himself between us. This is an example of an unsuccessful collaboration.

What are three things you have learned about the theatre?

1. Those who run it are timid, fearful people whose good intentions are usually subverted by economic realities.
2. Critics are scum.
3. Audiences are terrifying.

What are three things you have learned about playwriting?

1. The joy and the anguish that goes into the creation of the text is a pretty good reason for living.
2. Everything that comes after that is no fun at all.
3. "Success" is an infinitely relative concept that recedes like Zeno's Arrow and owes vastly more to timing and connections than it does to talent.

How do you, as a playwright, build relationships with theatres and other theatre artists?

Man, are you ever asking the wrong guy.

What was the most helpful piece of advice you ever recieved about working in the arts? Who gave it to you?

Be kind to the people you meet on the way up because you'll meet them again on the way down: Broadway folk wisdom.

What piece of advice would you share with emerging theatre artists?

Read, listen, observe, and never mistake your opinions for Universal Truths.

RINNE GROFF

Rinne Groff is a playwright and performer. Her plays, including Jimmy Carter was a Democrat, Orange Lemon Egg Canary, Inky, The Five Hysterical Girls Theorem, *and* The Ruby Sunrise, *have been produced by the Public Theatre, Trinity Rep, Actors Theatre of Louisville, PS122, Target Margin, Clubbed Thumb, and Andy's*

Summer Playhouse, among others. Ms. Groff is a founding member of the Elevator Repair Service Theater Company and has been a part of the writing, staging, and performing of their shows, both in the United States and on European tour, since the company's inception in 1991. She was trained at Yale University and New York University's Tisch School of the Arts.

How do you measure a "successful" collaboration?

When embarking on any project, of course, I dream of "success" in all the tangible (which basically means materialistic) ways: big houses for the production, nice reviews, support from the community that is producing the work. All these things are important, and as I am engaged in making something for the public to enjoy, I am susceptible to relying on all the well-trod signs that my show is well regarded by the public I am writing for. However, there have been times when the good reviews and sold-out audiences have not come, but I still feel grateful for the collaboration and the work process. Why? Usually it involves working with someone from whom I've learned a lot: a director or a composer, a producer, or sometimes an actor with whom I feel I've made a connection. So I think to myself, yes, that project didn't accomplish everything I'd hoped it would but (1) I got to share time with a person who has so much to teach and give, and (2) maybe we'll get to continue our collaboration on other projects in the future. Additionally, if I feel like I've learned a new skill or been exposed to a different side of myself (for example, if the project was my first musical, or my first adaptation), that, too, can make the collaboration feel like a success, just because I know I am walking away from the experience with more than I went into it with: more knowledge, more confidence, more compassion.

What are three things you have learned about playwriting?

1. Story is everything.
2. Keep touching base with "what's the story here?" Never lose sight of it.
3. Because story is everything.

What was the most helpful piece of advice you ever received about working in the arts? Who gave it to you?

Shortly before I had a play opening, which was my biggest play opening to date, I was a nervous wreck. I was so pleased with the work, mine and the designers and the actors and the director, but I was dreading the reviews coming out. All these people around me were saying, "This is it. This is your greatest play. This is your big break. This is where you take off." And it was only making me more and more unhappy. Finally I talked about it with my director. Why does the support and good wishes from all these people only make me miserable? (And I really was crying intermittently but persistently in this period). And my director said to me, "It's making you miserable because it's subscribing to the one-big-break model." He said, "I've been working in this business for thirty years (actually, I can't remember the number he said), and I've never had 'the big break.' You don't have to subscribe to that mentality. You can keep making work and find success without ever having the break-out play."

His words really helped me and I was able to refocus on the work at hand instead of "would such-and-such a review make me or break me." And the reviews came out, and they were mixed, and I survived, and my career survived, and I still treasure what he told me.

JEFFREY HATCHER

Broadway: Never Gonna Dance (*book*). *Off-Broadway*: Three Viewings, Scotland Road, The Turn of the Screw, Neddy, Tuesdays with Morrie (*with Mitch Albom*), *and* Murder by Poe. *Cincinnati Playhouse*: Scotland Road, The Turn of the Screw, Everything's Ducky (*with Bill Russell and Henry Krieger*). *Mr. Hatcher's other plays include* To Fool the Eye, Mercy of a Storm, Korczak's Children, One Foot on the Floor, Pierre, The Servant of Two Masters, The Fabulous Invalid, *and* Work Song (*with Eric Simonson*). *Theaters that have produced Mr. Hatcher's work include Manhattan Theatre Club, Primary Stages, The Old Globe, Yale Rep, The Guthrie, Milwaukee Rep, Philadelphia Theatre Company, Actors Theater of Louisville, City Theater, Children's Theater Company, South Coast Rep, Oregon Shakespeare Festival, Alabama Shakespeare Festival, Florida Stage, Florida Studio Theater, Repertory Theater of St. Louis, Missouri Rep, Arizona Theater, Portland Stage, Denver Center, Intiman Playhouse, The Empty Space, and many others in the United States and abroad. His film adaptations include Stage Beauty, directed by Richard Eyre and starring Billy Crudup and Claire Danes, and Casanova, directed by Lasse Halstrom. He is writing films for directors Steven Shainberg (Secretary) and Kim Pierce (Boys Don't Cry). He has written for the Peter Falk TV series Columbo and has won grants from the National Endowment for the Arts, Theatre Communications Group, and the Lila Wallace Fund; he has received the Rosenthal New Play Prize, the Frankel Award, and other awards. A Picasso won Philadelphia's 2003 Barrymore Award for Best New Play. Mr. Hatcher is a member of New Dramatists, The Playwrights' Center, WGA, and the Dramatists Guild.*

How do you define collaboration?

I win all the arguments except the ones that make my work look better.

How do you measure a "successful" collaboration?

A successful production, which isn't necessarily the same as happy collaborators.

How do you measure an "unsuccessful" collaboration?

The show stunk.

What are three things you have learned about the theatre?

1. Bravery is almost as important as talent; talent without bravery will lead to capitulation or compromise.
2. Choice of director and cast constitute 90 percent of a play's chance for success.
3. The person who finds a way to crack the power of the chief critic for *The New York Times* will be made a God.

What are three things you have learned about playwriting?

1. The structural planning you do before you sit down to write is more important than the actual writing.
2. Character comes first, before theme, before language, before plotting.
3. I'm still learning my craft, a realization that is both debilitating and heartening.

How do you, as a playwright, build relationships with theatres?

It's fairly easy to figure out whether a theatre and its audience are sympatico with your work. If it's a bad fit, you'll find out after one shot. It's good to get along with the artistic staff—in terms of personal relationships—but the real relationship is with your plays. Initially, your first play sent to the theatre is your calling card. If that play is accepted and produced, and it succeeds, chances are you'll do another. Sometimes an artistic director likes a playwright's sensibility and gives him a chance on something unknown—a commission for a new work or adaptation—and their hopes are founded on past experience with his work. I try to keep in good contact with the theatres I think will be receptive to my work, and not badger them about scripts I think are outside their interest. But, as much as I like to get along with people, I know of few theatres that keep a playwright around because he or she is charming or fun to be with (that's how actors are chosen).

How do you, as a playwright, build relationships with other theatre artists?

I try to keep in touch with colleagues, but I'm not overtly social, nor am I a big joiner of organizations, clubs. I don't network. It's exhausting. I like writing people. Email was personally designed for me.

What was the most helpful piece of advice you ever received about working in the arts? Who gave it to you? What piece of advice would you share with emerging theatre artists?

The answer is the same: Lloyd Rose, who was then literary manager at the Arena Stage in Washington, D.C., sent me a rejection letter that included this line: "While there was much in your play to recommend it, in the end we did not feel compelled to produce it." That's the only reason theatres should produce plays: they have to, or they'll die. Take that to heart, Grasshopper.

J.T. ROGERS

J. T. Rogers' latest play, The Overwhelming, had its world premiere in 2006 at the National Theatre of Great Britain; upon the completion of its initial run it will tour the United Kingdom. His Madagascar received the 2005 Pinter Review Prize for Drama for best play in the English language and has been published in hardback through the University of Tampa Press. The play also won the American Theatre Critics Association's 2004 M. Elizabeth Osborne Award and was a finalist for the ATCA's Steinberg New Play Award. It was seen in 2005 Off-Broadway as part of the SPF Summer Play Festival. Rogers is the author of White People (nominated for best play of the year by the L.A. Drama Critics Circle, Barrymore Award of Philadelphia, and the Carbonell Award of South Florida), Seeing the Elephant (Kesselring Prize nominee for best new American play), and Murmuring in a Dead Tongue, which was presented last season in New York City by Epic Rep, where he is a company member. Regionally, his works have been given full productions at the Philadelphia Theatre Co., New Actors Union Theatre (Moscow), the Road Theatre (Los Angeles), New Theatre (Miami), the Adirondack Theatre Festival (NY), and many times at the Salt Lake Acting Co., where he was a 2004–2005 NEA/TCG playwright in residence. Rogers has been an artist-in-residence at the Eugene O'Neill Theater Center and the Edward Albee Foundation, and was the recipient of a 2004 playwrighting fellowship from New York Foundation for the Arts. He lives in Brooklyn.

How do you define collaboration?

Working with a director and actors who trust each other and have checked their egos at the door, where we are all focused on making the play (not the playwright) as good as possible.

How do you measure a "successful" collaboration?

The play is much better when the collaboration is finished than when it started.

How do you measure an "unsuccessful" collaboration?

I haven't had one yet. And feel lucky to be able to be able to write that.

What are three things you have learned about the theatre?

If everyone likes what you are doing, you are doing something wrong; the process is the point of what we do, the product is only something that the process inevitably leads to; judge people in our field by what they do and not what they say, as this will teach you whom to trust.

What are three things you have learned about playwriting?

If I am convinced that no one other than me will ever be interested in something I am interested in writing about, that is what I need to be writing about; it is impossible to write something good with less than a year's work; when writing, start your scenes late, and get out of them early.

How do you, as a playwright, build relationships with theatres?

That is not a question for a writer, but for a theatre. There is not a playwright in this country that would not, or does not, write better, quicker, and with more daring when a theatre says, We want to have a relationship with you—i.e., we will do your work. Anything short of that is not a relationship, it is only casual dating. And no party ever gets any long-term meaning from casual dating.

How do you, as a playwright, build relationships with other theatre artists?

When I see or read a play that knocks me for a loop, I seek out that writer to see if they want to have coffee and talk about writing. (That is, if they'll return my phone call.)

What was the most helpful piece of advice you ever received about working in the arts? Who gave it to you?

One day in rehearsal for The Crucible in college, the director, my acting teacher Marty Rader, said to me: "What makes this day different than any other?" Later, in response to my question of whether I should play a scene this way or that way, he answered: "Which choice is more useful?" As a writer, asking myself those two questions has helped my work immeasurably.

What piece of advice would you share with emerging theatre artists?

At a certain point in your writing/directing/acting process, you need to ask yourself the following question: is what I am doing going to pass the Time+Money test? That is, will what I am creating be worth the time (four-plus hours) and money (theater tickets, babysitter, dinner out) of my audience members? The best way I know to answer that in the affirmative is to make work that asks questions of an audience that they don't already know the answers to. If you honestly look at your work and it is not doing this, why shouldn't people stay home and watch HBO instead? If what you are working on does not pass this test, be pleased that you have learned to judge your work so honestly, go back to drawing board, and take perverse comfort in what Samuel Beckett had taped over his writing desk: "Fail, fail again, fail better."

LISA DILLMAN

Lisa Dillman's plays have been produced in Chicago at Steppenwolf, American Theatre Company, Rivendell Theatre Ensemble, and Collaboraction; in New York at Hypothetical Theatre Company; in Santa Fe at Theaterwork; and elsewhere around the country. Six Postcards was featured in the Goodman Theatre's 2005 New Stages Festival. Lisa has received the Sprenger-Lang New History Play Prize, the Sarett National Playwriting Award, and the Julie Harris–Beverly Hills Theatre Guild Award, as well as two commissions from Steppenwolf, two playwriting fellowships from the Illinois Arts Council, and residencies at the Millay Colony, the Ragdale Foundation, Blue Mountain Center, and the O'Neill Theater Center, where her play Rock Shore was workshopped in the 2003 National Playwrights Conference. Her plays are published by Dramatic Publishing, Smith and Kraus, Heinemann, and New Issues Press. Lisa is writing a new play commissioned by Rivendell Theatre Ensemble.

How do you define collaboration?

Artists working together, stimulating and challenging one another repeatedly on their way to the common goal of creating something amazing.

How do you measure a "successful" collaboration?

Whether the eventual product succeeds or fails, I measure a successful collaboration by the level of talent, commitment, willingness, and honesty the collaborators bring to the process. I measure it by the extent to which everyone is working toward the same goal and willing to take risks within that framework. And, partly, I measure it by the willingness to explode the framework if that's what it takes to create the best art.

How do you measure an "unsuccessful" collaboration?

For me unsuccessful collaborations seem to come in two basic forms. One is the "too-nice" form where all the players compromise far past their comfort zones and the project ends up a sort of Frankenstein monster put together out of spare parts. The other is the "me-first" form where one or more collaborators cleave so rigidly to their own ideas—the ones they walked in the door with—that there is a lot of argument and endless discussion, but no real spirit of teamwork or momentum. Of course, each collaborator brings something special to the process, something unique and individual. But for me the most intense and productive moments in a collaboration tend to evolve from my sudden understanding of a brilliant idea that came from someone else. In new play workshop and development situations I find myself constantly learning new things from actors, directors, and dramaturgs about the play I wrote. In production situations, designers sometimes provide me with huge revelations, both by their approach to the work and by the questions they ask.

What are three things you have learned about the theatre?

Audiences are smart.
Audiences love a great story.
I'd rather be offended or infuriated than bored.

What are three things you have learned about playwriting?

Write for the brightest people in the room, and never underestimate the audience.

I attempt to listen carefully to every bit of feedback I get on my work. I don't have to use it—it's *my* play—but I at least pay attention and try to absorb it.

The craft of playwriting is an ongoing learning process. I hope to God I still feel like I'm learning about it for the rest of my writing life.

How do you, as a playwright, build relationships with theatres?

I read a lot and see a lot to get a fix on where my work potentially fits in with a theatre's mission and goals. When I run across a theatre that is doing great work, I try to meet and get to know people who are involved with that company.

How do you, as a playwright, build relationships with other theatre artists?

I try to meet and get to know other artists whose work excites me. I do a lot of connecting by email. I go to other writers' readings and productions. In Chicago, where I live and work, the theatre community is very tight-knit. There's a lot of support among writers, which is definitely part of why I love it here.

What was the most helpful piece of advice you ever received about working in the arts? Who gave it to you?

My grandmother, who was not an artist, used to tell me, "The race is long, and in the end it's only with yourself." I have thought of that statement so many times over the last however-many years of working in a competitive and increasingly marketing-driven profession. I've learned that it's absolute death if I start benchmarking my own career against the careers of other playwrights. Writing requires a tremendous amount of time spent battling it out in solitude. It can be painful, and then really thrilling, and sometimes just grueling. So I think at base you have to love doing it, the discoveries and the process, and the transitions from head and heart to page and from page to stage.

What piece of advice would you share with emerging theatre artists?

Work hard. Stay open and learn as much as you possibly can.

Don't be an asshole.

Be generous with your colleagues.

Cultivate enthusiasm.

Be patient.

GINA GIONFRIDDO

Gina Gionfriddo has received an Obie Award, a Guggenheim Fellowship, The Susan Smith Blackburn Prize, The Helen Merrill Award for Emerging Playwrights, and an

American Theatre Critics Association/Steinberg Citation. In addition to Philadelphia Theatre Company, After Ashley has been seen at Actors Theatre of Louisville, The Vineyard Theatre Company, and Woolly Mammoth, and will be seen in spring 2007 at Denver Theatre Center. The play has been published by Smith & Kraus and is forthcoming from Dramatists Play Service and Limelight Editions in Best Plays 2004–2005. *Other plays include* U.S. Drag *(Connecticut Repertory Company and Clubbed Thumb, New York, directed by Pam MacKinnon) and* Guinevere *(The Eugene O'Neill Playwrights Conference). She is a graduate of Brown University's MFA Playwriting Program and has taught at Brown University and Providence College. Currently, she is a staff writer for the NBC drama,* Law and Order: Criminal Intent.

How do you define a "successful" collaboration?

A successful collaboration with a dramaturg for me happens when the dramaturg commits to the play the playwright is trying to write. I think it's fine in the beginning to say, "I think it would be fascinating if the play took on x, y, and z" but once the playwright has really clarified what she wants to accomplish, I think the dramaturg needs to let go of goals for the play she and the playwright don't share. The times I have really thanked God for my dramaturg have been in rehearsal rooms where actors and directors either try to rewrite the play or attack the morals or ethics of the characters. It is vital to have, in these times, a dramaturg who can oh-so diplomatically steer us back to the play and out of Oprah-land—discussions of who in the play is right and good versus who is wrong and bad. Also. There is a tendency as a play approaches production, for directors and producers to advocate "Band-Aid" or "panic" rewrites—taking lines away from the weakest actor, cutting time off the play because actors aren't up to speed. It's vital in these times to have one person (dramaturg) whose priority really is the play, not the production.

How do you define an "unsuccessful" collaboration?

I have, fortunately, not had many. My one horrible experience, interestingly, was having my play dramaturged by another playwright. And the issues there were, as alluded to above, an agenda for a different play than the one I was writing. Also, I think there are times when a writer needs a breather from notes and feedback and a good dramaturg respects this without feeling rejected, keeps taking notes, and holds them until the writer feels ready to hear them. I also feel strongly that the dramaturg should be the playwright's ally and keep the dialogue private, so that any reservations or problems the dramaturg finds in the play are not revealed to the actors while they are laboring to commit to the words.

What are three things you have learned about the theatre?

1. No one wants to be the first. If one theatre produces you, four others will make you an offer. Ditto on commissions. There is tremendous cowardice in decision-making in institutional theatre.

2. The time is past for hyperrealism on stage—faucets that run, ovens that cook. Film and TV do it better. If theatre is to survive it must be theatrical.
3. Criticism and consumer advocacy are very confused right now.

What are three things you have learned about playwriting?

1. Write the scene you're longing to write, even if you think it's the third scene in the second act. If you are writing towards the thing that excites you instead of writing what excites you, it's probably dull writing.
2. Have fun! If you aren't enjoying what you're writing, no one else will. And you don't get paid enough to feel miserable when you write. (There are plenty of paying gigs for that!)
3. Write for the peers you respect. Writing for critics and subscribers and audience is poison. Think about that playwright whose work amazes you and write the play they will want to see.

How do you, as a playwright, build relationships with theatres?

I have built relationships with theatres through dramaturgs and literary managers who like my work. I focus on those dialogues that feed me. I honestly don't think hobnobbing and "networking" get you anywhere. I think relationships are formed on the basis of work and it's not an issue of good work versus bad work. For me, it's been a matter of which literary managers and dramaturgs and associate producers spark to my work and get it and want more.

How do you, as a playwright, build relationships with other theatre artists?

I have built relationships with other theatre artists through graduate school at Brown and the O'Neill Theatre Center. The decline of the O'Neill is a longer, sadder discussion. I was lucky enough to spend two seasons there and I am not overstating the case to say that Jim Houghton and a handful of playwrights I befriended there are the reason I kept writing plays. Some of these writers—Adam Rapp, Cusi Cram, Brooke Berman—are my best friends now and I truly do keep them in mind when I write because they are writers writing for the right reasons, not as a stepping-stone to TV, not to win a Tony. Playwrights need to keep an eye to why the thing they write is a play—not a novel, not a movie. It's vital to have writers and dramaturgs in your life who are theatre purists that way. That's not to say don't write for TV. I love writing for TV! But theatre is so hard—heartbreaking and bank-breaking—you have to really stay focused on why it's necessary.

What was the most helpful piece of advice you ever received about working in the arts? Who gave it to you?

Christopher Durang told me to be careful in rewriting that you don't gut the play of its soul. He said that he's seen interesting plays cleaned up and clarified to the point where they were sanitized and unremarkable. Sometimes within a play's mess is its magic. That's not license to be lazy, but it's a great bit of caution. Along similar lines, Erin Cressida-Wilson has questioned contemporary dramaturgy's focus on "clarity," seeing ambiguity and self-contradiction as error to be corrected. This is so important, I think. In *After Ashley*, for example, the "Julie" character sticks around while another character (Justin) is quite cruel to her. And I have heard repeatedly in rehearsal rooms, "I would never do that" and "no woman would do that." Of course, that's insane. Humans do all variety of things you and I would never do and theatre *has to* put that onstage. That's one of the main ways we distinguish ourselves from film and TV! Hollywood development is all about making characters more "accessible." When theatre excites me, it shows me how and why we do those "inaccessible" things.

What piece of advice would you share with emerging theatre artists?

Grad schools you don't have to pay for are an amazing way to get out of the work force and really write for a couple of years. Listen to your instincts about what it takes for you to write. Maybe "write every day" isn't for you. Maybe your method is to work like crazy at a money job (or two or three) for six months and then stop working altogether and write until you need to work again. It was very hard for my parents to see me nanny after they'd financed my college. They wanted me in an office doing something they considered cerebral. But office work and writing were a bad match for me. Be at peace with the raised eyebrows from family, etc., who think childcare, waitressing, cleaning houses is beneath you. It's not. Listen to yourself.

NICK WARDIGO

Nick Wardigo's plays include Chessboard Heroes, The Biggest Box of Crayons, *and* Editorial Decisions. *He has received the Roger Cornish Award as well as fellowships from the Pennsylvania Council on the Arts and the Pew Fellowships in the Arts.*

How do you define collaboration?

Of all the "writing arts," playwriting is clearly the most collaborative. A professional playwright doesn't write anything without thinking about her actors, director, stage manager, costume designer, lighting designer, and so on. Novelists take direction from their agents and editors, but playwrights need to collaborate right from the gate, because if the play isn't stageable, it's crap. Once the play is accepted, it's input from everybody. The director, dramaturg, and actors, obviously, but sometimes even the stage crew can offer good advice about, say, how reworking a plot element will make things easier for the prop guy.

How do you measure a "successful" collaboration?

A play that works. That's difficult to measure. For a comedy, you can go by the number of laughs. For a drama, it might be dependent upon comments in the lobby or maybe repeat business. Reviews are worthless in this regard (but potentially very helpful for the box office). Mostly, you just know; you either know it works or you know it doesn't.

How do you measure an "unsuccessful" collaboration?

A play that doesn't work. It falls flat, doesn't move, doesn't keep the interest of the audience, doesn't excite, doesn't inflame, doesn't inspire, doesn't offer insight, doesn't make you think, doesn't make you feel.

What are three things you have learned about the theatre?

1. Theatre is a business, which means it has a bottom line.
2. Almost everyone connected with a theater for any length of time is very competent at their job...they just don't look that way.
3. With rare exceptions, actors can't write, playwrights can't direct, and directors can't act. The processes are completely different; most plumbers have no idea how to extract teeth.

What are three things you have learned about playwriting?

1. You have to love all of your characters. You don't have to like them, or agree with them, but you have to love them.
2. Don't try to make a point. Just write the damn thing.
3. Minimize dialogue. If you can write a scene without a single word, do it.

How do you, as a playwright, build relationships with theatres?

I attend shows to see the sorts of things they produce. If possible, I read their mission statement in their program or on their website. Then I try to meet the decision-makers (literary managers or artistic directors or whatever) in a casual setting. I find the Barrymores [Philadelphia's awards program for the theatre] are good for this. Even better, I like going to public readings. Literary managers are much more relaxed in this sort of environment, and because we just watched a play-in-progress, they're in a "play development" frame of mind and very open to conversations of what they're looking for and how to submit a script.

How do you, as a playwright, build relationships with other theatre artists?

I buy them drinks. I listen. I learn about their professional problems, what they like and dislike, what they like to see in a playwright, what pissed them off about their last production.

What was the most helpful piece of advice you ever received about working in the arts? Who gave it to you?

I'm paraphrasing, but it was something like, "Theater isn't literature. Don't try to write flowery prose. Just write what the characters are saying." Playwright Jeffrey Sweet told me that.

What piece of advice would you share with emerging theatre artists?

Plot is easy; characters are hard. If you can't hear your characters, you don't know them well enough. I like to write "practice dialogue" until I understand their world views as well as their idiosyncrasies and vocal tics. Once you have the characters down, you can just toss them in a room together, and a plot will emerge organically.

TRACY LETTS

Tracy Letts saw the world premiere of his play, Bug, *in 1996 at the Gate Theatre in London, which was followed by the American premiere at A Red Orchid Theatre in Chicago and a wildly successful run off-Broadway at Barrow Street Theatre, where it ran eleven months for a total of 384 performances, before closing in 2005. In addition to* Bug, *Tracy Letts is also the author of the critically acclaimed plays* Man from Nebraska *(named by* Time *magazine as one of the top ten plays of 2003 and a Pulitzer Prize finalist) and* Killer Joe. *Mr. Letts is an ensemble member of the Steppenwolf Theatre Company (Chicago), where he has appeared in* Homebody/Kabul, The Dazzle, Glengarry Glen Ross, Three Days of Rain, *and* Picasso at the Lapin Agile. *His film credits include* Guinevere, U.S. Marshall, *and* Chicago Cab *and his television credits include* The District, Profiler, The Drew Carey Show, Home Improvement, *and* Seinfeld. *Mr. Letts recently made his directorial debut at the Looking Glass Theatre with Glen Berger's play,* Great Men of Science, 21 & 22.

How do you define collaboration?

A process in which more than one person is encouraged to contribute.

How do you measure a "successful" collaboration?

The finished product contains ideas of more than one contributor.

How do you measure an "unsuccessful" collaboration?

The finished product stinks. (The "process in which more than one person is encouraged to contribute" failed to produce aesthetically pleasing results.)

What you have learned about the theatre?

1. There is no excuse for boring an audience.
2. Movies and television simply cannot produce the visceral impact of live theatre.
3. As a playwright: If they're laughing, they're listening.

4. As an actor: Just because they're *not* laughing doesn't mean they're *not* listening.

What are three things you have learned about playwriting?

1. I have learned never to censor myself in the writing process.
2. I have learned that, in performance, my play will not look like what I see in my head—invariably, it looks better.
3. I have learned not to start the actual writing until I have considered the play for a very long time...years, in fact.

How do you, as a playwright, build relationships with theatres?

I've never had a play done because I sent a theatre a script. I've only had plays done as a result (or by-product) of doing my plays myself, holding readings, workshopping.

How do you, as a playwright, build relationships with other theatre artists?

Every relationship I have in the theatre has been created by working in the theatre. There is no excuse for not working.

What was the most helpful piece of advice you ever received about working in the arts? Who gave it to you?

I don't know the answer to that, but I can tell you the *worst*, or perhaps most misleading piece of advice I ever received. "You have to treat it as a business," or, "It's called show *business*," etc. One does *not* have to treat it like a business. I think this advice is an invitation to consider one's work, as well as one's role in the world, as a "product" or "commodity." I think it devalues the contributions of artists.

What piece of advice would you share with emerging theatre artists?

1. Read more fiction.
2. Stop apologizing. Look people in the eye and say, "Yes, I am an artist." This culture wants to tell you that artists are less than essential to the world, when in truth, we perhaps have never been more needed.
3. Tell stories. Worry about everything else later. *Tell stories.* At any given performance of any given play, there will be someone in the audience who has never been to the theatre before. Please ensure that person will return to the theatre. *Tell that person a story.*

AUSTIN PENDLETON

Austin Pendleton has written three plays, all of them published: Orson's Shadow *and* Uncle Bob (*both published by Dramatists Play Service*) *and* Booth (*Samuel French*).

He is also an actor (in theatre, film, and television) and a director (in theatre, of both new plays and established ones.) He teaches acting at the HB Studio, and directing at the New School, both in New York City, where he lives.

How do you define collaboration?

I don't define it. I try to let it be different every time.

How do you measure a successful collaboration?

When nobody cares who has had what idea.

How do you measure an unsuccessful collaboration?

When the work that comes out of it has no specific identity or texture.

What are three things you've learned about theatre?

1. That every play is different.
2. That every production of a given play is different.
3. That any production of a given play is finally about the combination of people who are doing it and where they are in their lives at that moment.

What are three things you've learned about playwriting?

1. That an audience will give themselves to anything if they are kept curious about what's going to happen next, at every moment.
2. That this can't really be achieved without characters who break free from the themes and biases of the piece and live on their own.
3. That every moment has to be active and therefore actable.

How do you, as a playwright, build relationships with theatres, and with other theatre artists?

I'm not a useful guide to this because I'd already built up so many such relationships from being an actor and a director.

What's the most helpful advice you got about working in the theatre?

That the most important thing, finally the only important thing, must be the work itself, always.

Who gave it to you?

Herbert Berghof, Anna Sokolov, Uta Hagen, Bobby Lewis, Olympia Dukakis, Nikos Psacharopoulos.

What advice would you give emerging theatre artists?

That same advice.

CHRISTOPHER SHINN

Christopher Shinn was born in Hartford in 1975 and lives in New York. He has received grants from the NEA/TCG Residency Program and the Peter S. Reed Foundation. He has received commissions from the Royal Court Theatre, the Soho Theatre (London), South Coast Repertory, and the Mark Taper Forum. He studied writing with Tony Kushner, David Greenspan, Maria Irene Fornes, Michael Cunningham, Richard Howard, John Dias, and Jessica Hagedorn. He is a graduate of the Greater Hartford Academy of the Arts High School and a former member of Youngblood, Ensemble Studio Theatre's young playwrights group. Presently, he is a member of New York Theatre Workshop's Usual Suspects and the Vineyard Theatre Community of Artists. His plays include Four, Other People, The Coming World, What Didn't Happen, Where Do We Live, Sleepers, *and* On the Mountain.

How do you define collaboration?

A collaboration is what happens when a group of people gather to carry out a common task.

How do you measure a "successful" collaboration?

A successful collaboration is marked by respect and passion—in other words, love.

How do you measure an "unsuccessful" collaboration?

An unsuccessful collaboration is marked by individuals pursuing their own goals at the expense of the collective task.

How do you, as a playwright, build relationships with theatres?

I try to write plays whose quality and power cannot be denied.

How do you, as a playwright, build relationships with other theatre artists?

I try to be a good, interesting, and gentle person that others wish to collaborate with.

What was the most helpful piece of advice you ever received about working in the arts? Who gave it to you?

"Know yourself." Tony Kushner.

What piece of advice would you share with emerging theatre artists?

Know yourself.

TOM DONAGHY

Tom Donaghy is the author of the plays The Beginning of August, Boys and Girls, Minutes from the Blue Route, *and* Northeast Local, *among others. He recently adapted* The Cherry Orchard *for Atlantic Theater Company. His plays have been produced by some of the most prestigious theaters in the country including The Atlantic Theater Company, The Goodman Theater, La Jolla Playhouse, Lincoln Center Theater, Playwwrights Horizons, and South Coast Repertory. Among his commissions and honors, Donaghy is the recipient of grants from the NEA, TCG, and the John Simon Guggenheim Foundation.*

How do you define collaboration?

A mutually respectful process by which theatre artists come together to create a meaningful event for audiences.

How do you measure a "successful" collaboration?

The above-mentioned process without the screaming. Or passive aggressive manipulation. Or silent suffering of any of the artists because they've been beaten into submission by egos greater than theirs.

How do you measure an "unsuccessful" collaboration?

If there's screaming. Also if the balance of power tilts any one way. That's usually toward the director. Directors, who are often lovely people, get to do several plays a year so they are a little (unconsciously for the most part) intoxicated by their own presence in the mix. Consequently they are overconfident and underprepared (they are coming from the last thing, going to the next thing), no matter how lovely they are over drinks. This means they are often playing in the dark, which terrifies them, so they will make decisions based on ego and fear without truly engaging the playwright because the playwright (the director knows in his/her heart) really does know more about the play. Even, God knows, designers can skew a collaboration disastrously. Usually these are Tony-award-winning designers with cavernous loft/work spaces in midtown Manhattan.

What are three things you have learned about the theatre?

1. Until playwrights can be trained and empowered to direct their own plays, theatre will be stuck in an antiquated, ineffective paradigm.
2. There are very few good producers, alas, who can create the correct context for a successful collaboration.
3. It takes forever to get a play on, and when it finally comes to pass a bunch of almost strangers are thrown together for six weeks' time during which they are expected to create something not only coherent but transcendent. Then it takes two years to write another play, and two more years to get it produced, at which point the cycle repeats.

What are three things you have learned about playwriting?

1. The so-called development process is by and large harmful.
2. Every playwright does it differently, so take all advice cautiously.

3. It involves a lot of tuna noodle casserole, pain, terror, and disappointment with intermittent flashes of joy that are enough to keep a true masochist hooked.

How do you, as a playwright, build relationships with theatres?

I try not to (see above). When it does happen it's because I keep up with what the theatre is doing, email staff members when appropriate, and make play dates with dramaturgs. Also, when I finish a new play I send it to the lit people and artistic directors whose opinions I respect. Readings are good, if they aren't completely cold and I can be involved in casting. It's a kind of first date. But I must always remember to be coy and not jump in bed without condoms and/or mace.

How do you, as a playwright, build relationships with other theatre artists?

I try not to. Wait, do you mean professionally? Similar answer to above question. I keep track of who's doing what, keep abreast of people's work, engage them in discussions about it—which they seem to appreciate—and drop notes, emails to convey what I appreciate. These things have always been meaningful to me when I've been on the receiving end.

What was the most helpful piece of advice you ever received about working in the arts? Who gave it to you?

Every day do something—one thing, however small—to better secure your place in the arts (theatre). A Pulitzer Prize–winning playwright gave it to me.

What piece of advice would you share with emerging theatre artists?

I'd say, "must you?" There are so many ways to enjoy theatre and life, are you utterly sure you want to so entangle the two? If they still insisted on emerging I would counsel them to start their own company, however informal or amateur. This would allow them to discover the particular individuality of their work—be it acting, directing, writing—and that of their peers. And also to discover in a practical, grounded way how their work comes to life on the stage. Not in the audition studio, or in classes, or in their dream. A company would also give them community, which is essential in a field that is dire, lonely, and punishing, and kill the pervasive notion among young theatre artists that they must be called to make theatre by an imagined "other" that has all the power. I'd tell them they could start making theatre *now* if they really wanted to. God help them.

JOSE RIVERA

Puerto Rican–born Jose Rivera's plays have been seen nationally and internationally and translated into seven languages. Rivera's plays have been performed at the Joseph

Papp Public Theatre, Playwrights Horizons, South Coast Rep, the Goodman Theatre, the Mark Taper Forum, Actors Theatre of Louisville's Humana Festival, Hartford Stage Company, and Manhattan Class Company—as well as theatres in Mexico, Puerto Rico, Peru, Scotland, Greece, Rumania, Sweden, Norway, England, and France. They include the Obie Award–winning plays Marisol and References To Salvador Dali Make Me Hot, as well as Cloud Tectonics, Each Day Dies with Sleep, The Promise, The House of Ramon Iglesia, Giants Have Us in Their Books, The Street of the Sun, Sonnets for an Old Century, and Sueno. His work has been generously supported by the Kennedy Center Fund for New American Plays, the National Arts Club, the NEA, the Rockefeller Foundation, the New York Foundation for the Arts, the Fulbright Commission, PEN West, the Whiting Foundation, and the Berilla Kerr Foundation. Rivera has studied with Nobel Prize winner Gabriel Garcia Marquez at the Sundance Institute and has been a writer-in-residence at the Royal Court Theatre, London. Television credits include cocreating and producing the critically acclaimed NBC series "Eerie, Indiana" as well as "The Eddie Matos Story" for HBO; episodes of "Goosebumps," "The Great Brain," and "Night Visions" for the Henson Company; "The Brothers Garcia" for Nickelodeon; and "A.K.A. Pablo" for ABC. Films include The Jungle Book: Mowgli's Story, Mr. Shadow, and Family Matters, all for Disney, as well as the 3-D IMAX film Riding the Comet for Sony. Current theatre and film projects include School of the Americas and Brainpeople (both commissioned by South Coast Rep), Adoration of the Old Woman (commissioned by La Jolla Playhouse), and the films A Bolero for the Disenchanted (Showtime), Somewhere in Time, II (Universal Home Video), The Motorcycle Diaries (Robert Redford's Wildwood Co. directed by Walter Salles), Lucky (Interscope), and Cesar Chavez (Showtime).

How do you define collaboration?

Listening. Never respond with "no" until all options are fully explored. Mutual respect. Admitting limitations in yourself and filling your weaknesses with someone else's strengths. Opening yourself up to unexpected ideas. Celebrating the creativity of another. The melding of complimentary visions.

How do you measure a "successful" collaboration?

You can't tell where one artist stops and another begins. You haven't murdered your partner.

How do you measure an "unsuccessful" collaboration?

A dead partner.

What are three things you have learned about the theatre?

It directly links you, no matter how old you are, to your childhood.
It will endure no matter how much technology is invented.
It has an endless power to break your heart and that's not always bad.

What are three things you have learned about playwriting?

It's the best drug.
You do get better the more you do it.
It has an endless power to heal you.

How do you, as a playwright, build relationships with theatres?

Stay on their A list, which is completely arbitrary and beyond your power to control.

How do you, as a playwright, build relationships with other theatre artists?

Travel.

What was the most helpful piece of advice you ever received about working in the arts? Who gave it to you?

Marcia Shieness, a New York playwright from the 1970s, once told me to not take any writing advice from anyone who didn't have a vested interest in my future.

What piece of advice would you share with emerging theatre artists?

Think in lifetimes, not in years. Don't rush yourself. Don't read about your more successful rivals. Be an information sponge. Go to your darkest place and live there honestly for a while. Don't try to be trendy. Don't try to be a German expressionist. Live cheap. Live in a foreign country. Learn languages. Read Chomsky. Read Rilke. Read Borges. Study the soul.

TRACEY SCOTT WILSON

Tracey Scott Wilson is the winner of the 2004 Kesselring *Prize for playwriting and the 2004* Whiting Award, *both for* The Story, *as well as the* Van Lier *Fellowship and the 2001* Helen Merrill Emerging Playwright Award. *Her other work includes* I Don't Know Why That Caged Bird Won't Shut Up, Exhibit #9, *and* Leader of the People. *Wilson holds a Master's degree in English literature from Temple University. The* Story *was first produced at the Joseph Papp Public Theater in December 2003 in a coproduction with the Long Wharf Theatre.*

How do you define collaboration?

Collaboration is when I allow others to help me shape, define, redefine, or edit my text to create theatre.

How do you measure a "successful" collaboration?

A collaboration is successful when my vision and the vision of the other collaborators are not polluted by politics or personality or power struggles. It is when discussion comes from a place of artistic vision instead of ego, pride, or power.

How do you measure an "unsuccessful" collaboration?

When ego, pride, and fear creep into conversations that should be about artistic vision.

What are three things you have learned about playwriting?

1. Writing a play is very hard.
2. Playwriting is all in the telling.
3. The economic realities of theatre make writing a play from pure imagination very hard.

How do you, as a playwright, build relationships with theatres?

My agent does a lot of work in that department. But usually someone sees a play and tells someone else and so on and so on and so on. The more you have readings and shows the more people get to know you and your work. It really is a grapevine.

How do you, as a playwright, build relationships with other theatre artists?

I meet artists at writer's retreats or parties given by theatres. From there friendships develop, phone numbers are exchanged. It's a small world in New York.

What was the most helpful piece of advice you ever received about working in the arts? Who gave it to you?

The only way to know where a line is, is to cross it. And what is life if nobody is crossing the line. You just want to try and be on the right side of history. Sometimes what is going on in the present is not as important as the long term. The truth is permanent. Everything else will fall by the wayside. (I heard Dave Chappelle say that in an interview. I wrote it down and taped it to my computer.)

What piece of advice would you share with emerging theatre artists?

Do what you love and the rest will follow.

JON KLEIN

Jon Klein is the author of over twenty produced plays, produced off-Broadway and at many prestigious regional theatres, including the Humana Festival at Actors Theatre of Louisville, Arena Stage in Washington, D.C., Arden Theatre in Philadelphia, Center Stage in Baltimore, South Coast Repertory in Costa Mesa, Alliance Theatre in Atlanta, Alley Theatre in Houston, A Contemporary Theatre in Seattle, Seattle Children's Theatre, and many others. Produced plays include Suggestibility, Wishing Well, Dimly

Perceived Threats to the System, Octopus, Betty the Yeti, Peoria, Southern Cross, T Bone N Weasel, The Einstein Project (*coauthored with Paul D'Andrea*), and Losing It. *He has also written several adaptations, including the exclusive stage version of the popular children's book* Bunnicula, *premiering at Seattle Children's Theatre along with two adaptations of the Hardy Boys book series. Other plays for young people are currently in process for both Seattle Children's Theatre, and the Kennedy Center.*

Jon's stage version of Stendhal's classic novel The Red and the Black *was produced at ACT Theatre in Seattle. Jon adapted* T Bone N Weasel *for a Turner Network film, starring Gregory Hines and Christopher Lloyd. Awards for other screenplays include the UCLA Showcase, the Zaki Gordon Memorial Award, and the George Burns and Gracie Allen Comedy Award. He has also three National Endowment of the Arts Fellowships and* Dimly Perceived Threats to the System *was a finalist for the American Critics Theatre Award. Jon has been a playwright-in-residence at the American Repertory Theatre in Cambridge, and the Alliance Theatre in Atlanta. He has taught playwriting and screenwriting at UCLA, the University of Texas, the University of Washington, Ohio University, and Hollins University. He is currently the head of the MFA Playwriting Program at Catholic University of America in Washington, D.C.*

How do you define collaboration?

Quite simply, working as a playwright is automatic collaboration, from the moment your script leaves your hands and is given to an actor, director, or designer. Then you necessarily enter into a series of discussions about the best methods of developing and staging that play, in consultation with others.

How do you measure a "successful" collaboration?

It always helps to be working with people who are curious about the playwright's intention, and who ask a lot of questions. And who express some enthusiasm about the project.

How do you measure an "unsuccessful" collaboration?

You can tell an unsuccessful collaboration in advance, the minute people say any of the following: "I have my own ideas about this play, so I don't necessarily need to hear yours," "This part doesn't work. You have to cut/change/edit it before we even try it," and "It's best if you don't come to rehearsal, but if you must, please don't say anything." Hopefully, these conversations will occur *before* rehearsal begins, so you can either request new personnel, or cancel the show.

What are three things you have learned about the theatre?

1. To quote screenwriter William Goldman, "Nobody knows anything." Which I interpret to mean, if you have preconceived notions, someone is bound to prove them wrong.

2. Be ready for anything. Don't be afraid of the unexpected—almost everything that happens, good or bad—can be useful, if you're prepared to use it.
3. Always be moving forward. Your hit play can sell out, win awards, and get the best reviews of your life. Don't sit by the phone waiting for those Broadway or film producers to call—they probably won't. Instead, pull out your legal pad, typewriter, or computer keyboard, and write "Act One." Start again.

What are three things you have learned about playwriting?

1. If it reads well on the page, it may not play well onstage. If it doesn't read well on the page, it may work brilliantly onstage. You just can't tell a thing until you hear the play out loud.
2. Something playwrights and actors share—personal misperception. People will assume you're just like the characters you write, or the roles you play. And they always become disappointed when they find out otherwise. You'll resent this at first—but you better learn to accept it. That's not going to change.
3. To quote Ernest Hemingway, "The first draft is always shit."

How do you, as a playwright, build relationships with theatres?

Once you get your foot in the door at one theatre, either through workshop or production, word of mouth can take over. The national theatre community isn't quite as communicative as it was in the 1980s (the peak period for emerging playwrights), but some folks do still talk to each other. A workshop at one theatre may lead to a production at another. And once you do have a relationship with a theatre, try to maintain it by sending scripts, attending events, and generally making a pest of yourself. This, too, is more difficult than it used to be, since artistic directors seem to have much shorter job tenures. Joe Papp, Jon Jory and Gordon Davidson had playwright relationships that lasted twenty years or more. Those were the days.

How do you, as a playwright, build relationships with other theatre artists?

See the above. Outside professionally sponsored events, it's difficult to approach people you want to work with or learn from, without seeming like a stalker. Go see their shows, attend their readings, then approach them afterwards. That's much better than calling them at home during dinner.

What was the most helpful piece of advice you ever received about working in the arts? Who gave it to you?

My late agent, Lois Berman, said it to me after a disastrous review: "No one remembers. People forget." And she was right.

What piece of advice would you share with emerging theatre artists?

Seek out a group of like-minded people that you don't mind working with for a few years. This is how New Dramatists, the Playwrights' Center, Steppenwolf Theatre, and Theatre de la Jeune Lune all got started (to name a few).

MELANIE MARNICH

Melanie Marnich's plays include Quake, Blur, Tallgrass Gothic, Beautiful Again, The Sparrow Project *and* Cradle of Man. *She has received two Jerome Fellowships and two McKnight Advancement Grants through The Playwrights' Center, the Samuel Goldwyn Award, and the Francesca Primus Prize, was a finalist for the Susan Smith Blackburn Prize and an L. Arnold Weissberger Award nominee. Her work has been seen at Manhattan Theatre Club, Steppenwolf Theatre, the Actors Theatre of Louisville, the Guthrie Theater, and Dallas Theatre Center. Commissions include the Guthrie, the Kennedy Center, Arena Stage, and La Jolla Playhouse. She is a Core Member of The Playwrights' Center and a member of New Dramatists.*

How do you define collaboration?

Tough question to kick off with. For me, the essence of collaboration lies in a generous exchange of ideas and energy. A process in which everyone is invested, but no one is guarded or territorial. For collaboration, the biggest ego in the room needs to belong to the project—not the people. Everyone is gathered in service of the project and to giving their all without being proprietary or precious. It's really a bunch of people in a room with their shirtsleeves rolled up.

How do you measure a "successful" collaboration?

Perhaps this sounds selfish, but for me, a successful collaboration is one in which a script evolves during a process with actors, directors, dramaturgs (or any combination of the above), while it remains connected to its heart and its core impulse. I tend to think a process like this is successful when it doesn't judge the play but still manages to rigorously test it to see if it holds water. I want a collaboration to take me and my writing to a place I couldn't get to while working alone. And I want the play to be examined and explored for what it is and what it has the potential to be. I love it when the people in the room look to what works—rather than what doesn't work—and then start from there. It's such a constructive, productive feeling.

How do you measure an "unsuccessful" collaboration?

Well, in my experience, these have been situations in which people focused on what wasn't working and set about trying to fix it. That has never worked for me, as it seems to lock the process into a negative mind-set. If the play then winds up as a completely different creature from the one it was at the start of the process, it typically has gone off course for me. I lose my connection to the work. And at the end of the day, I'm the one who has to live with it long-term.

What are three things you have learned about the theatre?

That it is necessary.

That I am always a beginner in it.

That it is wonderfully terrifyingly chimerical and that I can never count on it treating me the same way two days in a row.

What are three things you have learned about playwriting?

That no play I write will ever feel finished to me—but that I have to learn when to say "done."

That while I avoided focusing on fundamentals such as plot and structure early in my career because I thought I was more "organic" a writer than that— these things are the backbone of the most rewarding theatrical experiences one can have (or can give an audience). And they're *hard* (maybe that's why I avoided them?). Now I know that if I really want to take an audience on a great ride, if I really want to give them their money's worth, I have to have my story in place and know how to tell it well. I can write as "organically" as I want, but without solid plot and structure, my play won't be as effective as I need it to be. Period.

That I make my discoveries about writing *while* I'm writing, not while I'm waiting to write. I used to wait till lightning struck. Funny how it strikes a lot more when I'm actually at my desk.

How do you, as a playwright, build relationships with theatres?

I'm a lousy networker. I become friends with all these terrific theatre people at all these terrific theatres, then I think, "Oh, I can't send her my play, I know she's really busy . . ." I seem to have a very hard time blending the personal and professional. I'm learning to be more practical about it and to not sit home writing, thinking my agent or my plays will do the networking for me. It's ultimately my responsibility. Recently, I've started to make a point of sending my scripts out and staying in touch with people I've met over the years. It's not easy, but it's necessary. I try to cultivate friendships and to stay on top of what the theatres I admire are doing.

How do you, as a playwright, build relationships with other theatre artists?

I've had the good fortune to be based in Minneapolis and to be connected to The Playwrights' Center there. That's like having an instant community. The writers I've met through the Center have all been similar in that we manage to all be very ambitious, but also very supportive of each other. I like to read my friends' plays, see their shows, cheer them on. On a more national level, I've developed great relationships by working on my plays at various festivals and workshops and being part of the teams that get assembled in those environments. So often, I've been blessed with superb collaborators and friendships and professional relationships have evolved from that.

What was the most helpful piece of advice you ever received about working in the arts? Who gave it to you?

"Look at all the people in the audience who are enjoying your show—and ignore the rest." My mom gave me that.

What piece of advice would you share with emerging theatre artists?

I like to tell students of mine to always maintain a sense of perspective and balance, to stay connected to the world outside of theatre, otherwise it will make you crazy. Because ultimately, it's make-believe, isn't it? It's capricious and subjective and whimsical. If you're looking for one plus one to always equal two, theatre isn't the right place for you. I think it's so important to look up from the page, the stage, whatever, and take in what's going on around you. A broader perspective will feed your soul and your art, and keep you sane. A life in theatre is inherently filled with highs and lows. Find your stability elsewhere. We can all be crazy in the short term, but if someone really wants to be in this for the long haul, sane is the only way to go.

LARRY LOEBELL

Larry Loebell's most recent play, La Tempestad, *was performed at the Ohio Theater in Soho in 2005. Other plays include* Girl Science, The Ballad of John Wesley Reed, The Dostoyevsky Man, *and* Memorial Day. *From 1998 to 2005 Larry was the literary manager and dramaturg at InterAct Theater Company in Philadelphia. Larry teaches narrative film history at the University of the Arts, and playwriting and dramaturgy at Arcadia University. He is a four-time recipient of the Pennsylvania Council on the Arts Playwriting Fellowship, has received an EST/Sloan Foundation rewrite commission, and was recently awarded a National Foundation for Jewish Culture grant to research his next play in Israel.*

How do you define collaboration?

Director and playwright on the same wavelength about the play. Simple as that. Working in tandem toward the same ends. Two of the three equity productions I have had (the world premieres) were effortless for me because I believed in the director and we had a good give and take about all issues artistic and dramaturgical. Didn't always agree but always felt that the points of view came from the same source—really seeing the play clearly. The third was a nightmare because I felt the director was wrong about every impulse and I was too inexperienced to know how to take the play back. The director got her way and it was a disaster. I think this is also about knowing your director well enough to know that he/she has the right impulses and is on the right wavelength. This may be the best reason to do workshops.

How do you measure a "successful" collaboration?

I would say that if both the director and I get to the end of the process and feel our artistic aims have been served by the production, the collaboration is successful.

How do you measure an "unsuccessful" collaboration?

When I feel the director isn't listening, has a vision he/she wants to impose, when I feel we are not on the same wave length, the collaboration is not successful—even if the audience sees an okay product.

What are three things you have learned about the theatre?

1. Everything takes forever to happen.
2. Everything costs more than you think it will—in human, emotional, and actual capital.
3. For me, whatever the costs, I am really not happy anywhere else. Theatre is my church and community. It is where I am most significantly connected to the world. Except for my family, of course.

What are three things you have learned about playwriting?

1. No play is ever entirely finished. There are just interim drafts.
2. You can always go deeper.
3. Tragedy needs sex and laughter.

How do you, as a playwright, build relationships with theaters?

I send plays with literate letters. Hang out with dramaturgs. Write lots of queries. Try to see plays and talk to ADs of theatres I am interested in when I travel. Ask theatres to sponsor me for grants. Try to get my name out there in various ways, including by being on list serves and in online chats. Urge my agent to make introductions.

How do you, as a playwright, build relationships with other theatre artists?

I see a lot of theater. I try to try new things when I can, especially locally, to work with companies that work in different ways than I am used to. I go to see performers I am interested in. I have a very robust correspondence, a lot of it to other artists.

What was the most helpful piece of advice you ever received about working in the arts?

This is a hard question for me because I came to real work in theatre very late in my life. I was forty-seven. Before that I took the more conventional advice: get a job, have a career. I worked in film and television, mostly on the commercial production side of the business for twenty years. When my kid was out of college and married I walked away from all that at the urging of my wife, who was, fortunately, well employed. She probably gets the nod here. She told me: this is not a rehearsal. This is your life.

You want to be a playwright and dramaturg—go do it. Screw the economics. Gotta love advice like that.

Who gave it to you?

Diane A. Loebell, Esq.

What piece of advice would you share with emerging theatre artists?

Pretty much the same advice—without the promise to support them economically. If you want to do it, do it. Learn your craft, be open to whatever comes, take chances, but do it.

EVAN SMITH

Evan Smith's plays have been produced in New York by Playwrights Horizons, the Lincoln Center Director's Lab, the New Group, and the Home for Contemporary Theatre at HERE. Beyond Manhattan, his plays have been at theaters at the Yale Cabaret and 1812 Productions, Philadelphia. He recently worked with Fox TV and a production company on an evening of one-act TV pilots. His plays are published by Grove Press, Dell Books, TCG, Smith & Kraus, the Dramatists Play Service, and Playscripts.com. Smith taught scriptwriting at the Savannah College of Art and Design, and was recently an outside mentor for the Yale Playwrights Festival. He attended Vassar College and the Yale Drama School.

How do you define collaboration?

Collaboration happens when multiple people work to one end. In the theatre it happens when all the people who are working on a production of a play (a) have the same artistic vision and (b) have the same marketing goals. ("Marketing" is my catchall word choice for the money side of theater.) Successful collaboration is more often sabotaged by problems arising out of (b) than (a). This is because practical concerns impact artistic decisions, and marketing is the area where the goals of the different major collaborators on a production are the most disparate. The commercial producer wants to sell tickets; the artistic director wants the schedule to be on time; the director and playwright both want their part of the production to further their careers—whatever their career goals may be. If the perfect actor is unavailable in September, but scheduling at a resident theatre requires that rehearsals begin September 15th, what to do is a collaborative decision. If an actor has been miscast, but must be endured, does one allow her to do what she can do well, protecting her but skewing the story, or does one push her to do what the story requires, helping the story, but opening her up to harsh criticism? Collaborative decisions like these often impact the different collaborators differently.

The ideal of perfect collaboration is a lovely and heartwarming aspiration that can be used to bludgeon playwrights into a bloody pulp.

Because collaboration can be so mind-bendingly wonderful when it goes well, tradition declares that the ideal must be protected at all costs. This is done by demarking the areas of responsibility of the different collaborators. Any infringement of the different territories is considered a violation of the spirit of Art herself. But, the true definition of collaboration says that all participants should be aiming at the same artistic vision. If various participants do *not* have the same vision, collaboration by definition is a dead duck, and the gloves should come off.

A director once said to me, "You've got to trust me." We were in a restaurant, surrounded by new acquaintances, so I did not vent my anger. I do not feel like I have to "trust" anybody, especially not—as in this case—a director whose work I knew almost nothing of. Many or most collaborations for beginning playwrights are like blind dates ending with mandatory unprotected sex. The truth of theater collaboration is that all the details are or should be covered by contracts. There is nothing in the contract that says a playwright has to hand over—in the name of "collaboration"—the entire physical production to the director. If the director appears to have a contrary artistic vision, fight back. Fire the director if you have to. Be prepared to take over. Learn how to talk to actors. Don't let artistic directors or producers intimidate you.

Keep in mind that the vast majority of directors work mainly on classic plays or licensed productions of recent hits—where the playwright is not in any way a player. They are trained to put their own stamp on a play, often in defiance of performance tradition or the playwright's well-known intention. This fact has created a situation where many directors think the playwright's contribution ends when the play spools out of the printer, that the design process and the rehearsal hall are both the exclusive province of the director. They are wrong, and the only way to handle them is to let them know from day one that you fully expect every one of your whims to be realized on stage at least to the extent that the director's are.

Here's a little bit of advice that speaks obliquely to the great myth of collaboration: don't go into theatre to make friends. Make friends with accountants, web designers, teachers, or journalists. Too often show-folk (consciously or unconsciously) value friendship over artistic excellence, and emotionally manipulative arguments of loyalty and friendship can be wielded disastrously in artistic conversations.

How do you measure a "successful" collaboration?

Money.

How do you measure an "unsuccessful" collaboration?

Getting a critical drubbing for artistic decisions I did not sign off on, or perhaps even fought against tooth and nail.

What are three things you have learned about the theatre?

1. Theatre is as full of compromise as movies and TV.
2. There is no such thing as an exclusively "popular" hit in the realm of non-musical theatre. Rob Schneider can thumb his nose at the movie critics and get on with his career. No playwright has the same luxury with regard to the theatre critics (and I extend the term "theatre critic" to include the foundation grants, fellowships, residencies, etc.).
3. There are forces in theatre today that reserve the highest rungs of artistic achievement in writing exclusively for those playwrights who produce not traditional plays, but who instead provide "texts" that can be adapted for the stage by directors. These "plays" are what the wider world calls "poems." The resulting theatrical events are sometimes moving, and the productions visually arresting, but a work that has no characters and no stage directions is not a play. Beware directors who fancy themselves authors.

What are three things you have learned about playwriting?

1. There is a real disconnect between what critics say they like and what they actually like. For example, critics use words like "subtle" to describe plays they like, so playwrights respond by writing subtle plays, only to be eviscerated for writing "aimlessly" or "shapelessly." Upon further research, the playwright discovers that that "subtle" critical hit is actually as ham-fisted as Bill O'Reilly at Lilith Fair. To save psychological wear and tear, ignore what people say about what they like, and examine closely the actual text.
2. Words and ideas always take a back seat to story shape. There is no way around this.
3. Anybody attempting to give you notes on a play should be allowed to do so only by referencing the structure and *not* the content. If you have written a play about a mother and a son, for example, do not get suckered into having long conversations about the nature of mother/son relationships. This is counterintuitive, but important. Living people need psychological solutions; plays need theatrical solutions. If somebody tries to teach you about or change your mind about your themes and ideas, tell them to fuck off. Notes should sound like "Try to raise the stakes here," or "I wish there was more between Celia and Todd in Act II," or "The scenes are all sounding too much alike; it needs tonal variety." Bad, use-

less notes sound like, "What were you thinking when you wrote this bit?" or "I keep thinking of my mother when I was a child . . ." or "How about if she just gets so angry that she blurts out all the secrets—that way . . ." Avoid dramaturgs who employ the Socratic method; it's passive aggressive and worse than useless. Tell them to stop asking questions and just say what they have to say. Don't let actors (or anybody) give notes in the form of solutions, i.e., "How about we do this?!" Tell them to keep the solutions to themselves and just say what the problem is that needs solving You'll supply the solution when you're good and ready.

How do you, as a playwright, build relationships with theatres?

I don't; they build relationships with me—by producing my plays. When I get to the point where I am forced to choose between theatres competing for my plays, then I could think of myself as building relationships with them. That rather hostile caveat aside, I realized long ago it was the height of self-destructive stupidity to long to be produced at a theatre that had shown no interest in my plays, or had actually turned me down. It has never failed, in my limited experience, that the theatre in a given city that chooses to produce a play of mine is always the theatre the programming of which is closest to my heart, the employees of which are the most congenial company, and the actors and designers of which most closely reflect my taste. Generally speaking, I tend to like less the theatre made by the companies that don't do my plays. (Naturally, I limit this observation to those theatres that are roughly comparable to the ones that do produce my plays.)

Then, too—to get very specific about my own personal biography—my oeuvre is, I think, more than usually diverse, and I have repeatedly found myself in the position that Theater A, which produced Play A of mine and liked it very much, has no interest whatsoever in Play B, though they are maybe interested in Play C. Theater B, which produced Play B of mine, and quite liked it, has no interest in Play C or Play A. This has made building relationships very difficult, although I am just now getting to the point where I have relationships with a wide enough variety of theaters that I can find a home for each of my different plays.

How do you, as a playwright, build relationships with other theatre artists?

I don't. My experience as a playwright is still so limited and far-flung that the only people I think of myself as having working relationships with are artistic directors. They are the ones who end up making the hiring decisions.

What was the most helpful piece of advice you ever received about working in the arts? Who gave it to you?

Wendy Wasserstein once said to me, "The important thing is just to get the job."

What piece of advice would you share with emerging theatre artists?

When successful artists give guest lectures at art schools, they often say that artists can't create if they're thinking about audiences, critics, or success—that an author must write what comes from the heart, and if this is done faithfully, then success will follow. This is a lie. This is the dream of someone who became successful by thinking about audiences, critics, and success. Besides, what sort of audience? (Broadway tourists or readers of American Theatre?) Which critics? (Ben Brantley or Robert Brustein?) What kind of success? (Mac Wellman success or Terrence McNally success?) Opening your heart is only the first step in making art.

Know what you want to achieve and work to achieve it. One-set, four-actor plays get more productions than three-set, ten-actor plays. Realistic, traditional comedies don't tend to get published in American Theatre. Foundations often attach political strings to grants. If you cannot or will not adapt your work to suit your ambition, you must at least adapt your ambition to suit your work.

KIMBERLY SENIOR BAKER

Kimberly Senior Baker is the founder of Collaboraction Theatre Company and an Artistic Associate with Strawdog Theatre Company and Next Theatre Company. Recent productions include Three Sisters in a world premiere translation by Curt Columbus, Strawdog; Casanova, Collaboraction; Bold Girls, Seanachai; Patty Red Pants, Blackbird Productions; Mouse Cop, Noble Fool Theater; Fuddy Meers, Strawdog. She has directed for Maxwell Street Historic Preservation Coalition, Rivendell Theatre Ensemble, Shakespeare's Motley Crew, Northlight Theatre, Roadworks Productions, Northwestern University, College of DuPage, National Louis University, WFMT Radio among others. As a teacher, Kimberly is a resident artist with Steppenwolf for Young Adults where she directs the Teen Cross Town Ensemble and teaches in-school residencies. Kimberly has taught classes and/or run programs at Court Theatre, Roadworks Productions, Act One Studios, Redmoon Theatre, Victory Gardens, Audition Studio, Metropolis Center for the Performing Arts, and others. She last appeared on stage in Steppenwolf Theatre Company's No Place Like Home, for which she was also a contributing writer. She is the recipient of the 2001 Mercedes Mentor Award and was named one of the top five Chicago directors by New City in 2001.

How do you define collaboration?

Collaboration: an ongoing dialogue between people working towards the same goal where the sum is greater than its parts.

How do you measure a "successful" collaboration?

When all members of the collaborating team are empowered to work to their fullest potential because their work is enhanced by the work of others.

How do you measure an "unsuccessful" collaboration?

When it feels like "too many cooks spoil the soup," when egos get in the way, when people throw tantrums, and when no one seems to get anything done. Processes like these are usually marked by too many meetings and not getting anything actually done.

What are three things you have learned about the theatre?

1. It's in motion—nothing is ever "finished."
2. The best artists are often the best listeners.
3. It is too a real job.

How do you build relationships with theaters and other theatre artists?

Sharing in each other's work, opening up a dialogue with other artists about their work or theatre in general. I try to know whom I want to work with and seek them out, learn their work.

What was the most helpful piece of advice you ever received about working in the arts? Who gave it to you?

Not every problem needs to be solved by me—sometimes things need to go on the "List of Things That Are Not My Problem." It was given to me by my dear friend and mentor, Jessica Thebus.

What piece of advice would you share with emerging theater artists?

Don't be afraid to work for free, twenty-four hours a day. Be generous with yourself, time, and talent. You will get paid back.

LISA MCNULTY

Lisa McNulty is the Associate Director of Artistic Operations at the Manhattan Theatre Club. Prior to that, she was the Associate Artistic Director of the Women's Project, where she had the privilege of producing Lynn Nottage, Rinne Groff, Tanya Barfield, Caridad Svich, Anne Kauffman, Diane Paulus, Leigh Silverman, Neena Beber, Lisa D'Amour, Melanie Marnich, and many, many other incredible artists. Prior to that, Lisa was the Producing Associate at the McCarter Theatre, where she served as Line Producer for numerous mainstage and second stage productions including: Uncle Vanya, adapted and directed by Emily Mann; Yellowman by Dael Orlandersmith (2002 Pulitzer Prize finalist), directed by Blanka Zizka; The Tempest, directed by Emily Mann, starring Blair Brown; and Candida, directed by Lisa Peterson as well as McCarter's annual commissioned shorts series, which featured new work by Sarah Ruhl, Eric Bogosian, Polly Pen, Arthur Kopit, Alice Tuan, Ellen McLaughlin, and many others. Lisa was a founding member and Literary Manager for Zena Group, which premiered work by Mark O'Donnell, Jose Rivera, Neena Beber, and others.

How do you define collaboration?

For me, collaboration is about getting the right people in the room, and then shepherding them through the process in a way that allows everyone to do their best work. I feel like a midwife, mostly.

How do you measure a "successful" collaboration?

When the final product is greater than the sum of the abilities of any one collaborator.

How do you measure an "unsuccessful" collaboration?

When the personalities overwhelm the work. The work suffers and no one learns the lessons.

What are three things you have learned about the theatre?

Nobody makes enough money, there's never enough credit, and it twists people. Cynical, but true.

How do you build relationships with theatres and other theatre artists?

You have to make good work, be an interesting and pleasant human being, and put yourself in people's way. Eventually word will get around that you're someone worth knowing. Relationships in this business breed more relationships, so get to know as many cool, talented people as you can stand.

What was the most helpful piece of advice you ever received about working in the arts? What piece of advice would you share with emerging theatre artists?

1. Keep your goals in mind always—it's easy to get bogged down in the day-to-day details and frustrations of a life in the theatre, but if you don't keep a clear sense of where you'd like to end up, you don't have a snowball's chance in hell of getting there.
2. Unless you've got a Foremen-esque trust fund, find something non-theatre-related that people will pay you money to do (carpentry and computer-y things seem like good options) in order to pay your bills when you're starting out. Otherwise you'll get stuck in some administrative job at a theater, in hopes that it will connect you to an organization and make you some contacts (and a very little cash). All it will actually do is pigeon-hole you as "that guy who works in development" and make it harder for you to be seen as an artist. I've seen it happen to too many people.
3. Also, don't wait for someone to give you permission to make work—you should be making your own work all the time.

PAM MACKINNON

Pam MacKinnon most recently directed David Mamet's Romance *at the Goodman Theatre. Other recent projects include* After Ashley *at Philadelphia Theatre Company (where she also directed Edward Albee's* The Play About the Baby*) and* Bach at Leipzig *by Itamar Moses at New York Theatre Workshop. MacKinnon has also directed the world premieres of Edward Albee's* Peter and Jerry *at Hartford Stage,* Father Joy *by Sheri Wilner at CATF, and* 3F, 4F *by Victor Lodato at the Magic Theatre in San Francisco. She works frequently with Clubbed Thumb, Inc. where she is an Affiliated Artist, at New York Stage and Film, and the O'Neill Playwrights' Conference on new play development.*

How do you measure a "successful" collaboration?

Success is when all the little conversations between individual collaborators allow for the other ones to flourish and when the results of the little conversations—like a good play, itself—are surprising, yet inevitable. As I am a director, conversation is really all I have. There is no right and wrong, just the opportunity for better based on continued conversation.

How do you build relationships with theatres and other theatre artists?

Be persistent and polite. Remember that today's receptionist is likely tomorrow's decision maker, so be open to interesting conversations wherever you find them.

What was the most helpful piece of advice you ever received about working in the arts? Who gave it to you?

Don't confuse an opportunity with an accomplishment. Des McAnuff had just landed his first big-budget Hollywood film and was at once excited and very wary.

What piece of advice would you share with emerging theatre artists?

Don't confuse an opportunity with an accomplishment. There is much made these days in the business and political worlds of the distinction between players and workers. There are very, very few players in theatre outside maybe a couple agents and critics. Landing a job is just the start. Perhaps because of the freelance nature of a lot of people's lives, for some this ends up feeling like a goal. It can't be the goal.

AARON POSNER

Aaron is an adaptor, director, teacher, consultant, and cofounder and the Resident Director of Philadelphia's award-winning Arden Theatre Company where he has directed more than forty productions over the last eighteen years. His produced adaptations of literature include Who Am I This Time? *by Kurt Vonnegut, Jr.,* Right Ho, Jeeves *by P. G. Wodehouse,* The Brothers K. *by Fyodor Dostoevsky (with Terry Nolen),* Echoes of the Jazz Age *by authors from the 1920s,* Ellen Foster *by Kaye Gibbons,* Third & Indiana *by Steve Lopez, and* Brief Interviews with Hideous Men *by David Foster Wallace (with Scott Greer, Tony Lawton, and Michael Hollinger). His adaptation, with Chaim Potok, of* The Chosen *was originally presented by the Arden and Pittsburgh's City Theatre and won the 1999 Barrymore Award for Best New Play. It has since been produced by more than thirty theatres all across the country to nearly unanimous acclaim and sold-out houses. His latest adaptation,* A Murder, A Mystery & A Marriage: A Mark Twain Musical Melodrama, *will premiere this spring at the Delaware Theatre Company and the Roundhouse Theatre in Maryland. His upcoming adaptations include* Sometimes A Great Notion *by Ken Kesey, and another Chaim Potok novel,* My Name Is Asher Lev. *Aaron is also a freelance director with such theatres as The Folger Shakespeare Theatre, Actors Theatre of Louisville, Seattle Repertory Theatre, Alliance Theatre, Arizona Theatre Company, and many others. Directing awards include a 1998 Barrymore Award for* A Midsummer Night's Dream *at the Arden, and a 2005 Helen Hayes Award for* The Two Gentlemen of Verona *at the Folger Shakespeare Theatre in Washington, D.C. He is an Eisenhower Fellow, holds a BS in Performance Studies from Northwestern University, and is originally from Eugene, Oregon.*

How do you define collaboration?

Collaboration is just working together toward a common end. Defining it is easy. Doing it well, on the other hand, is hard. Very hard. And, for those of us who are not geniuses or auteurs, but rather hardworking theatrical craftspeople, it is also incredibly important. The quality of my collaborations are at the core of my success as a director and adaptor. I count on having good people around me to not only help achieve my vision, but to help challenge it, shape it, refine it. Collaboration is central for me.

True collaboration is a slippery slope. When artistic minds and temperaments come together and collide, energy is released, and that is excellent and full of endless potential. But this released energy can lead in a variety of directions. A really bad collaboration can mean finding yourself somehow working by committee and ending up with work that plummets to the lowest common denominator. That is the nightmare collaboration scenario. Great collaboration can mean a group bringing their best selves to the work, getting on the same page, pushing and inspiring each other, and finding new and better ways to take the work higher, further, and deeper than would have otherwise have been possible. Great collaboration, I find, takes the work to places that no one person on the team could even have conceived or accomplished alone. That kind of collaboration is truly thrilling and effective. Most collaborations fall someplace in between, I imagine.

How do you measure a "successful" collaboration?

It is always finally about what ends up on the stage. That is the final measure for me. Did it make the work better? That is the question. Even if the process is difficult, if it ends up truly making the work better then the collaboration has been successful. Of course, it is much more enjoyable if the process is fun and positive, at least much of the time.

But I increasingly think some degree of conflict and disagreement is an equally important part of a truly effective collaboration. Not that you should go out of your way to disagree, but if you bring your best and brightest self to the table along with other smart and passionate artists, then the chances are extremely high that not everyone will agree all the time, and I think that is great. I find that I want more smart, passionate conflict these days, not less. Good collaboration never loses sight of what you are working towards, but the collaborators cannot be afraid of a little trickiness or conflict along the path. Things need other things to bounce off of, to be seen in contrast or juxtaposition to. That creates energy and leads to innovation. Disagreements and complex and challenging discussions and explorations show you where you are coming from, where you just might be, and hopefully where you are going. That is both exciting and invaluable.

How do you measure an "unsuccessful" collaboration?

Did the work suffer because of the collaboration? Was it a miserable experience for me and for others? Did I learn new things? Do I feel richer or poorer for the experience? Those are some of the questions I ask. If the answers to too many of these are negative then it is an unsuccessful collaboration. And the first question is the most important.

What are three things you have learned about the theatre?

Oy, such a question. A question this large and wide can only reflect what is obsessing and engaging me about the theatre at this moment.

1. We, as human beings, want stories. We need stories. We need to hear great stories as we grow and learn about the world and about ourselves. We need to form ourselves as human beings in relation to the great stories. The need is there for what we do. And the onus is on us in the ever-struggling live theatre to keep doing what we do better and better, to reclaim ground that we have lost to the world of electronics.
2. We need to embrace and nurture complexity, in ourselves, in young artists, in our organizations, in our art, and in our audiences. Heart and mind, imagination and reality, passion and precision, talent and skill, comedy and tragedy, sameness and difference, hope and despair, faith and doubt, inspiration and provocation, good and evil, and on and on

and on. . . . We are living in complex times when the quality and tenor and complexity of public discourse is reaching an all-time low. I think we need to find better and better ways to embrace the endless complexity of human beings in all their wonder and weirdness—and we need to find ways to bring that to our work on stage.

3. Far too much work that is being done on our stages is either terrible, just plain bad, or at the very least not nearly good enough. With all of the challenges before us, our first and largest obligation is not to stink up the stage with work that does not astonish, connect, provoke, and truly engage audiences. While we definitely need places to grow and explore and experiment, we also need to put better and better work on our stages. Or our audiences will finally disappear . . .

What are three things you have learned about playwriting?

1. You need to have *something to say worth saying.* I think this is so important, and somehow so easily overlooked. This is why I, personally, adapt great literature by truly great authors. I honestly hope someday to have more to offer from my own life and experience, and then I will do my best to share it in an effective and hopefully beautiful way. But speaking as a reader and director, I am looking for playwrights that truly have something to say, and not just smart or clever and even highly theatrical ways of saying it. I am focused on work that is worthwhile. And by that I don't mean serious. Great joy and frivolous enjoyment can be highly worthwhile.

2. Don't be afraid of bad first drafts. Don't be afraid of it sucking for a while or you will never get anything done. It is so much easier for me to keep working on something and make something better. Something is so vastly better than nothing. I have to have the courage to let it suck for a while. Or else I would never start.

3. This is almost too cliché to say at this point, but. . . . Make sure whatever you are writing truly belongs in the theatre, and not on film, in television, in a book, on the radio, or wherever. That the theatre is perhaps the only place you might be able to get it produced is not a good enough reason. The theatre—more now than ever, with the absurd proliferation of all forms of electronic entertainment—must renew, revive, revitalize and reexplore those things that make it unique and truly able to draw in an audience.

How do you, as a playwright, build relationships with theatres?

Artistic Directors need to know you and know your work and there it is. It is that simple. How do you make that happen? Each path is different and there is nothing like a blueprint. I started a theatre, and thus had a place to refine my work as an adaptor and director and that gave me the opportunity to learn and grow. There are no set paths.

How do you, as a playwright, build relationships with other theatre artists?

Again, this is a little different for me because I am primarily a director, so I have built many of my relationships in theatre because I have found people whose work I really like and respect and I hire them.

What was the most helpful piece of advice you ever received about working in the arts? Who gave it to you?

"You know how you always are trying to raise the stakes on stage, because it makes the play or the scene or the moment more interesting and more engaging? The same is true of your life in this work. Raise the stakes, be bold, take real risks, and the payoffs will be greater and the adventure more exciting." That advice was given to me by Larry Sloan, the former Associate Artistic Director of the Goodman Theatre and Lincoln Center Theatre and Artistic Director of Remains Theatre in Chicago. I was trying to decide between suffering through two more years of a grad program that I was not enjoying, or moving to Philadelphia and starting a theatre with no money and no real professional experience. I heard him. I took the risk and raised the stakes. It went very well.

What piece of advice would you share with emerging theatre artists?

Three things:

1. I would pass on Larry's advice, as I have many times.
2. Be a mensch. Be a good, kind person. Be good to people. Be considerate and do the right thing whenever you can and try not to fuck people over. This business is very small, and very hard, and almost no one makes enough money and it is a struggle for most folks in one way or another most of the time. There is no place in it, in my opinion, for insanity and unkindness and backstabbing. So you will have choices to make when you may have to fuck other folks over a little, when you may really want to go back on your word, when you may have to make tricky judgment calls. Veer towards the kind.
3. Take the long view. Think more about questions than answers, at least until you are, you know, in your forties. It is a longish life, and things take time. Keep at it. If you are truly the very most talented, the very most brilliant, than maybe you can make it in a sprint. For most of us, it is more of a distance run. Take your time. Learn more, enjoy the questions, live in the questions, relish the exploration, learn who you are in the work and what you truly have to offer and then find the best possible ways of doing that.

RUSS TUTTEROW

Russ Tutterow has been the Artistic Director of Chicago Dramatists since 1986. At Chicago Dramatists, he has directed countless new play readings, and nurtured the art and careers of hundreds of playwrights. Most recently, he directed Chicago Dramatists' productions of Heat *by Marsha Estell,* Only the Sound *by Jenny Laird,* A Blue Moon *by Joel Drake Johnson,* Drawing War *by Brett Neveu, and* The Prophet of Bishop Hill *by David Rush. He currently serves on the First Look Council for Steppenwolf Theatre and recently directed Prop Thtr's acclaimed production of* Rosemary *by Jim O'Connor, which won 2002 Jeff Citations for New Play and Actress in a Principal Role. Mr. Tutterow has been involved in not-for-profit, commercial, and educational theatre for over twenty-five years. He has directed, managed, or taught for such Chicago theatres as Goodman, Victory Gardens, Royal George, Mercury, Briar Street, Prop, Zebra Crossing, Igloo, and Cullen, Henaghan & Platt Productions. He has held positions as Adjunct Associate Professor of Theatre at the University of Wisconsin, and Director of Theatre (for six years) at Lake Forest College in Lake Forest, Illinois. He holds an MA in theatre from Northwestern University and a BA in theatre from Ball State University.*

How do you define collaboraton?

It is different with each collaboration. The most important thing is for the parties, ahead of time, to talk through and agree on how they will collaborate and how they will behave in front of the other artists.

How do you measure a successful collaboration?

All parties still living at the end.

How do you measure an unsuccessful collaboration?

One of the parties is dead at the end.

What are three things you have learned about the theatre?

You do better work when you work with artists who are better than you.

You can't please all the people all the time.

There is only *one* unforgivable sin in the theatre: being *boring*. All other sins are forgivable.

How do you build relationships with theatres and other theatre artists?

Do your homework and show up in person.

What was the most helpful piece of advice you ever received about working in the arts? Who gave it to you?

Spend lots of quality time on the first things in the play. This is the foundation for the rest of the play and if you do that, the rest of the play will fall into place like magic. This has always worked for me and I now would never work any other way. This was said to me in my graduate directing class by Professor Richard Willis at Northwestern University in 1969.

What piece of advice would you share with emerging theatre artists?

See the last question/answer. And also: Perseverance!

LES WATERS

Les Waters won an OBIE Award for his production of Charles Mee's Big Love. *He directed its world premiere at the Humana Festival and subsequent runs at Berkeley Rep, the Brooklyn Academy of Music, Goodman Theatre, and Long Wharf Theater. He became Associate Artistic Director of Berkeley Rep in 2003, where he has also staged* Eurydice, Fêtes de la Nuit, Finn in the Underworld, The Mystery of Irma Vep, Suddenly Last Summer, *and* Yellowman. *Waters' work has been seen at theatres across the United Kingdom and the United States. In addition to* Big Love, *his New York credits include the Connelly Theatre, Manhattan Theatre Club, The Public Theater/New York Shakespeare Festival, and Signature Theatre Company. Elsewhere in America, he has directed for American Conservatory Theater, Goodman Theatre, Guthrie Theatre, La Jolla Playhouse, and Steppenwolf Theatre Company. In his native England, Waters has staged work with the Bristol Old Vic, Hampstead Theatre Club, Joint Stock Theatre Group, National Theatre, Royal Court Theatre, and Traverse Theatre Club. He has a long history of working collaboratively with prominent playwrights like Caryl Churchill and Charles Mee, and champions important new voices, such as Jordan Harrison, Sarah Ruhl, and Anne Washburn. Waters is an associate artist of The Civilians, a New York—based theatre group, and he headed the MFA directing program at U.C. San Diego from 1995 to 2003. His many honors include a Dramalogue Award, an Edinburgh Fringe First Award, a KPBS Patte, and several awards from the Bay Area Critics' Circle, Connecticut Critics' Circle, and Tokyo Theatre Critics.*

How do you define collaboration? How do you measure a "successful" collaboration?

When you want to work together again after the first collaboration.

How do you measure an "unsuccessful" collaboration?

See previous answer.

What was the most helpful piece of advice you ever received about working in the arts? Who gave it to you?

My mentor Max Stafford-Clark (then Artistic Director of the Royal Court Theatre in London) said, "If you don't like actors then don't do this." I remember at the time thinking that it was an extraordinarily patronizing piece of advice—of course I liked actors but so what? I was an assistant director at that point. It took me a long while to work out what he was really getting at. Which was actors are the ones out there doing it. They are the ones standing out there in front of people doing it. There are very few professions where you are encouraged to and often do fail in public. They risk failing in front of 400 people a night. So I'm now interested in productions (of many different kinds) where the performers own the production.

What piece of advice would you share with emerging theatre artists?

Always pay attention to the detail. It's the detail that counts. For directors: it's not your job to do everything. You can't act the play. You can't design it. You can't write it. You can have ideas and opinions but you presumably hired the team around you and you have to trust them to be able to do their jobs. If the writer writes the text then the director "writes" the production. And what I think is crucial is you have to be interested in the world you live in. What the politics are, who is writing what, what is going on in the visual arts. You need to pay attention, otherwise you're not going to grow.

JESSICA THEBUS

Jessica Thebus is an associate artist with Steppenwolf Theatre Company and an Artistic Associate at About Face Theater. Recent projects include About Face Theatre's Pulp *and* Winesburg, Ohio, A Midsummer Night's Dream *at the University of Notre Dame,* No Place Like Home *at Steppenwolf, an outdoor spectacle at the Field Museum,* They All Fall Down *at Lookingglass,* Seven Moves *at About Face,* Salao: The Worst Kind of Unlucky *with Redmoon Theatre (where she is a long-time collaborator),* Melancholy Play *by Sarah Rhul, and* Abingdon Square *by Maria Irene Fornes at the Piven Theater, where she is a long-time member of the teaching staff. Jessica has also directed at Center Theater, Lifeline Theater, Collaboraction Theater, and Caravan Productions, as well as touring internationally with the Bread and Puppet Theater. She holds a doctorate in Performance Studies from Northwestern University and has designed courses and taught at The University of Chicago, DePaul University, Columbia College, and Roosevelt University. She is currently a faculty member in the Directing Program at Northwestern.*

How do you define collaboration?

It is the central theatrical process, the only thing that makes it worth doing. The organic process that leads you to the thing you never would have discovered on your own.

How do you measure a "successful" collaboration?

The desire to work together again.

How do you measure an "unsuccessful" collaboration?

Not having that desire.

What are three things you have learned about the theatre?

Collaboration is at the heart of it. Be brave. Listen to others and the material as compassionately as possible.

How do you build relationships with theatres and other theatre artists?

Umm . . . very carefully? By working together. The relationship comes out of the project.

What was the most helpful piece of advice you ever received about working in the arts? Who gave it to you?

Antonio Sacre. He asked me, what would you do for free? Then that's what you should do for a living. Anna Shapiro told me to quit my job. And Frank Galati told me that triangles were the most interesting thing to look at.

What piece of advice would you share with emerging theatre artists?

Take and teach classes as often as possible.

LON WINSTON

Lon Winston is the Founding Artistic Director of Thunder River Theatre Company, located just outside Aspen, CO. He has directed, designed, or performed in well over one hundred productions. Lon has been a professor of theatre for over thirty years, twelve of which were on the Graduate Faculty at Villanova University. Lon's career has brought him in significant contact with some of theatre's most valued artists including: Zbigniew Cyncutis, Heinz-Uwe Haus, Jerry Rojo, Josef Svoboda, Megan Terry, Jiri Zizka, and with Sir Peter Hall and Dustin Hoffman in The Merchant of Venice. *From coast to coast, contemporary American theatre is being shaped by many protégés of Lon Winston, of which he is most proud.*

How do you define collaboration?

The true collaborative model is:

> Show up!
> Be present!
> Tell the truth!
> Let go of the outcome!

Of course, that doesn't always work in the theatre. Collaboration takes on a whole different look. However, I try to adhere to the true model. Letting go of the outcome means that one really allows the team to bring insight and help shape the vision. I trust the people I work with implicitly.

How do you measure a "successful" collaboration?

Everyone's willingness to do the above. To truly collaborate means to let go. It has to do with everyone involved on a production. Certainly a director and/or playwright need to have a sense of direction. That should actually happen before the collaboration begins. Once the collaborative process starts, then letting go of the outcome is essential. My dramaturg helps to shape and define the vision of the play. The actors collaborate to inform the characters and the action. The designers must certainly listen to the director, playwright, dramaturg, and hear and watch the actors, and then create the physical world of the play by bringing in their collaborative energy. In our theatre world, designers seldom have the opportunity to truly collaborate. They are usually asked to design a production before the play ever goes into rehearsal, one of the biggest travesties in the American theatre.

How do you measure an "unsuccessful" collaboration?

Too often collaboration in the theatre is perceived as—"I am the leader, and you collaborate with me to achieve my goals, vision, and desires." I believe that is a mistake in the theatre, especially when developing new work or building a theatrical piece.

What are three things you have learned about the theatre?

1. The actor is the one who is vulnerable in time and space, and all attention must be given to creating a world that makes the actor safe.
2. We cannot compete with film. Realism is just one of many "ism" filters that we see the world through. Therefore, we have an obligation to find the metaphors that allow the audience to come into the play, outside what many believe is the realistic norm.
3. There is life outside the theatre!

How do you build relationships with theatres and other theatre artists?

Through honesty, humility, hard work, follow-through, and thoroughness. Be the one to initiate dialogue. *Listen!* We have one mouth and two ears—use them in that proportion.

What was the most helpful piece of advice you ever received about working in the arts? Who gave it to you?

Believe in your team, and trust that they are colleagues and know as much as you. Told to me by my good friend and mentor, Jerry Rojo.

What piece of advice would you share with emerging theater artists?

Leave nothing in the theatre, ever, to arbitrariness.

Do not make any demands of anyone that you are not willing to demand of yourself.

CYNTHIA CROOT

Cynthia Croot is a theatre artist and activist living in Brooklyn. She earned her MFA in Directing from Columbia University and has staged dozens of productions ranging from classics to experimental new work in Alaska, Baltimore, Colorado, Chicago, and

New York City (Colorado Shakespeare Festival, Perseverance Theatre, Guggenheim Museum, New York's Town Hall, Symphony Space, etc.). She's directed such notables as Tim Robbins, Kathleen Chalfant, Joe Morton, and Marsha Mason, and has worked internationally in South Africa (Suzan-Lori Parks' Venus), Argentina (El Rayo Misterioso), and Austria. A guest artist at Whitman College, Bryn Mawr College, Columbia University, and Washington College, she's also an accomplished writer—awarded a Ucross Foundation residency for the script Mata Hari. Her play A Teacup Full of Vodka, based on the short stories of Anton Chekhov, premiered in Warsaw, Poland, in 2006. Croot pursues her humanitarian interests as a Firefly member (artists for Amnesty International), Steering Committee member of THAW (Theatres Against War), and U.S. delegate in an ongoing exchange between Columbia University's Center for International Conflict Resolution and the University of Damascus, Syria.

How do you define collaboration?

A woman I met this summer defined "peace" as a state that can be full of conflict, messy, challenging, and fraught—but in which no one gets killed. I think you can look at collaboration in a similar way. It could result in an ideological house getting burnt to the ground, but everyone can still go home to their own bed at the end of the day. If a collaboration is too polite, it probably isn't working. A healthy resistance makes things stronger.

How do you measure a "successful" collaboration?

One in which everyone involved learns something—and ideally, out of which something new is born.

What are three things you have learned about the theatre?

1. Why an artist makes work is as important as the work itself. You have to give a damn.
2. People who make great art can still be horrible human beings—but the measure of your life isn't whether or not you've had a hit show or developed new techniques—it's whether or not people are cheering at your funeral.
3. Deep, significant, resonant work takes time. A lot of time.

How do you build relationships with theatres and other theatre artists?

That's a great question. Trust them, I suppose.

What was the most helpful piece of advice you ever received about working in the arts? Who gave it to you?

Rick Davis told my class that if there was anything else we could do with our lives and be happy, we should do that instead. Robert Woodruff shared the quote that in theatre "elation can be your daily bread." It was good advice from both.

What piece of advice would you share with emerging theatre artists?

Be romantic. Be selfless. Be idealistic about everything you do. And never let anyone convince you otherwise. And find yourself a good secondary source of income.

PAUL MESHEJIAN
*Paul Meshejian is the Founding Artistic Director of PlayPenn, a national new play devel-
opment conference. Since 1989 he has served as a company member at People's Light &
Theatre Company (PLTC) outside Philadelphia where he has both acted and directed. In
addition to his work at PLTC he has performed with all of Philadelphia's major theatre
companies. He has been nominated for the Barrymore award numerous times. His work
has been seen on film and television. In the 1980s he was the Founding Artistic Director
of Stage One: Collaboration, a professional theatre in Minneapolis/St. Paul devoted to
new and rarely produced works. Paul is on the Acting Faculty at University of the Arts in
Philadelphia, also teaching at Arcadia University. He has a long history of new play development work as both actor and director in his fourteen-year relationship with The
Playwrights' Center in Minneapolis. He serves on the Board of Directors of the International Institute for Theatre Research and is a member of LMDA, Literary Managers and
Dramaturgs of the Americas.*

How do you define collaboration?

When I enter into any project with other artists and technicians and the project director has defined the work in such a way that all participants understand that we're in service to the play or whatever other form of text, etc. is primary—and that all participants in the room, including the leader, understand that the best idea in the room wins—that's when I consider I'm involved in collaboration.

How do you measure a "successful" collaboration?

I've always felt that a collaboration is successful if everyone involved feels that they've learned something along the way in the pursuit of something — something that ultimately has effect in the world and that winds up being, in some way unexpected.

How do you measure an "unsuccessful" collaboration?

When the end result of our agreed-upon work nets no progressive result—no new relationships, no deepening relationships, no new ideas or reconsideration of old ideas. Even if the product is not ultimately viewed as "successful," if there is an expansion of humanity in the process amongst those who are collaborating, then I count the effort as a success, though not on all counts.

What have you learned about the theatre?

1. Artists and audiences alike are far more enamored of an experience that asks them to make use of their imaginations than they are of costly and

usually doubtfully "imaginative" expressions by directors, designers, and other auteurs. Auteurs (not authors) are the antitheses of collaborators.

2. Progress is utterly dependent upon change. Even though it's arguable that there is nothing new in the world, change is, perhaps, our best substitute for "new." The theatre must constantly question itself on this idea and each of us must be insistent on change in order that the holy places stay vital to us and to our communities.

3. Art happens despite us, not because of us.

4. You can't tell anybody anything.

How do you build relationships with theatres and other theatre artists?

By meeting them on their terms, talking with them about their interests.

What was the most helpful piece of advice you ever received about working in the arts? Who gave it to you?

Keep thinking. My teacher and mentor, Sydney H. Spayde.

What piece of advice would you share with emerging theatre artists?

Train yourself for endurance. If you can think of something else to do, do it. If not, prepare yourself for a life of poverty and know that it's good taste and imagination that make for a desirable existence, not fame and fortune.

LEE DEVIN

Lee Devin graduated from San Jose State College in 1958 and took his PhD (1967) at Indiana University. He taught at the University of Virginia (1962–66), Vassar College (1966–70), and Swarthmore College (1970–2002). In 1970, he founded The Theatre at Swarthmore. An acting class in ensemble techniques, the first practical arts course offered for academic credit at the College, led eventually to an independent Department of Theatre Studies housed in a state-of-the-art building. He retired from teaching in 2002. In 1975 he became a member of the artistic staff of the People's Light & Theatre, acting, teaching acting, and doing dramaturgy. Along the way, he wrote articles, plays, opera librettos, and translations; worked as a technical director, master electrician, production stage manager, and dramaturg; acted and directed in the academy, the regional theatre, and for movies and TV. With Rob Austin of the Harvard Business School he wrote Artful Making: What Managers Need to Know about How Artists Work, *published in 2003 by Financial Times Prentice Hall. In 2005 it won LMDA's Elliott Hayes Award for dramaturgy. He's currently a dramaturg at People's Light & Theatre, and a Senior Research Scholar at Swarthmore College. He's at work on several writing and consulting projects, which interfere with, and cause him to neglect, his trout fishing.*

How do you define collaboration?

See *Artful Making*, p. 114 and elsewhere. When you define collaboration in your book, please be sure that you distinguish between collaboration and cooperation. Most of what folks call collaboration is in fact mere cooperation.

How do you measure a "successful" collaboration? How do you measure an "unsuccessful" collaboration?

These are nonquestions. You either collaborate, or you don't collaborate. The outcome of a collaboration may be successful or unsuccessful, but the work process is an either/or.

What are three things you have learned about the theater?

1. Acting is the second most fun thing you can do standing up. (I knew this before I knew the first thing.)
2. Dramaturg is the best job in the theatre. (I learned this in my fifties.)
3. Histrionic sensibility is the heart of what it means to be a human being. Use of language to make choices and suffer their consequences is the heart of what it means to have a human culture. Theatre is the art that celebrates these. (I figured this out just the other day.)

How do you build relationships with theatres and other theatre artists?

You work together. If your work is a collaboration, then you take parts of the other into yourself. You become, in part, each other. On a more superficial level: bind yourselves together with hoops of lunch. (*Polonius*. Those friends thou hast, and their adoption tried, / Grapple them unto thy soul with hoops of steel. . . .)

What was the most helpful piece of advice you ever received about working in the arts?

Don't look for helpful advice; there isn't any. By deciding to work as an artist, you have given up the luxury of having others help with or judge your work. If this leads you to arrogant disregard of others, you're probably not a theatre artist, but a very mere jerk.

Who gave it to you?

Figured it out for myself.

What piece of advice would you share with emerging theatre artists?

Stanislavski said, "Love the art in yourself, not yourself in the art." (This is not advice, it's a rule.)

SARA GARONZIK

Sara Garonzik has directed and produced, since 1982, for Philadelphia Theatre Company, which has introduced more than 100 world or regional premieres of major new American plays and musicals to Philadelphia including new work by Terence McNally, Jeffrey Hatcher, Christopher Durang, John Henry Redwood, Tracey Scott Wilson, Naomi Wallace, and Bruce Graham among others. In 1991 she was named to the PTC Board of

Directors. She also serves as a board member of the Arts & Business Council and the Theatre Alliance of Greater Philadelphia. Other service has included theatre panels for the Pennsylvania, New Jersey, and Ohio State Councils on the Arts as well as the Philadelphia Theatre Initiative, the O'Neill Playwrights conference, and as a judge for the 2005 Susan Smith Blackburn Prize. She is listed in Who's Who in American Women *and was named one of Business Philadelphia's "100 People to Watch." Bruce Graham sat down and interviewed her.*

Graham: Philadelphia Theatre Company (PTC) is dedicated to doing new plays. How many do you do in a season?

Sara Garonzik: We have a four-play season and it varies. This year we're doing two world premieres. Some years one.

G: Okay, let's say I'm a naïve young playwright—

SG: Yeah, right—

G: Who's trying to get produced at your theatre. How do I go about it? Where do those world premieres come from?

SG: A lot of places. Sometimes we follow a playwright's career. Playwrights we like or find interesting. And we'll approach them. "Please show us your next play." Of course we look at agent submissions or recommendations from other theatre professionals—other artistic directors. Sometimes a director we respect comes to us with a play they're passionate about. Sometimes scripts come over the transom—

G: You actually look at those?

SG: We do. That's why we have a literary manager. Somebody has to read those seven hundred scripts every year. You don't want to take a chance on missing that play that's right for you—that one-in-one-hundred shot that you want to support. Sometimes a producer will approach us with a play. They want a home for continued development, so we'll jump in at that phase. We've jumped in at every phase possible, from the commission—where it's not even written yet—to the commercial producer who has workshopped it and wants the first production.

G: The transom plays. The lit manager obviously can't read all of them, so do you have a system of readers?

SG: Oh yes. He has a whole system of readers.

G: Is there any hard and fast rule about what your theatre doesn't look for in a play?

SG: Absolutely. We tend to shy away from mysteries. Unfortunately, short plays, because it's difficult to create that context for a whole evening. Adaptations of European works, since we focus on American writers. I would say that includes modern "revisitations" of the classics. In other words, "*Electra*, set in contemporary Minneapolis." We just don't gravitate to something like that. But beyond that it's anything and everything. And in a way that's kind of a shame. That E*lectra* might be good, it's just not right for us.

G: After you put it over the transom, what then? What are the do's and don'ts? Without mentioning me by name, what's the worst thing a playwright can do?

SG: The worst thing you can do is submit a play in an unreadable format. Don't put in massive amounts of directions and descriptions. We're theatre professionals—we get it, we get it. I've read thousands of scripts. Trust us, we will be able to read it, no problem. The other bad thing is for a writer to call us every two weeks: "Did you read it?" It takes a while to get a play read—not just by one person but three people in this case—then form an opinion and write a response. It takes time. Anywhere from three to six months. So you've got to be patient. And never send us your last copy! We trust that you have downloaded or Xeroxed your script.

G: I always think of Eilert Lovborg in H*edda*. That clown had one copy of his manuscript.

SG: Well, that was a little before Xeroxing.

G: Writers actually do that?

SG: Believe it or not we'll occasionally get the writer who only has a few copies and ends up sending you the last copy and then is—of course—crazy about getting it back from you. So, submit it and be patient. I suppose it's okay to call every . . . oh, every third month. "Could you just update me as to where you are in the process?" Stuff like that. But make sure what you send is in the proper playwriting format. We get some plays that look like ransom notes. We want the most neutral presentation possible so that we can read it with the most open mind imaginable. So that nothing gets in the way of the content.

G: That's important about too many directions. My students often want to load it up. Every line has a suggestion as to how it should be read.

SG: I realize that Tennessee Williams was very concerned that the . . . oh, the tablecloth should be red, or something. But he could get away with it. Let it go. Trust us.

G: O'Neill did the same thing with his characters, but we can let him slide, too. Looking at a season—let's say you're doing two new plays and two established plays. Do you take into account a balance thing when choosing? In other words, we're doing two comedies so—

SG: Totally. Balance is everything—at least to me. A balance of theme, style . . . gender. You want a total journey for your audience from the first show to the last. You don't want anything that seems very familiar to the one that preceded it. You want to show them a banquet of possibilities. And with only four slots it can be tough because we want to show the whole array of the American theatre. We want to show what playwrights are working on now. Themes they think are important. We want to refute the feeling that, "Oh, they just do American plays." We want to show the infinite variety of the American writer. So we go out of our way to create an extremely diverse season.

G: So in looking at the total season—and I've had other artistic directors tell me this—you sometimes have to turn down a new play that you really like.

SG: Exactly! And you have to hope to God that the writer doesn't think you hate him. It has nothing to do with the quality of the play! But let's say I have a play that deals with female issues in a fairly realistic way—I can't have another one in the same season. So you bank it. I have a list of banked plays that I'd like to trot out at some other time.

G: Does having a subscription audience affect your choice? For instance, a friend of mine in Chicago loved *Coyote on a Fence* but was quite honest with me: "My audience won't go for it." Artistic directors have told me the same thing about *Belmont Avenue Social Club*. And when I was younger my first reaction was, "Screw 'em. If you like it, do it." But now I realize that you have to take that into consideration.

SG: Well, I like to think I'm kind of a "baseline" person. I'm not going to get too—I don't know, what's the word—I don't want to put myself above the audience as if to say, "I'm choosing this for you." Audiences don't know what they want until you show it to them. I like to think I show them what they want—that our tastes are similar. I like to think I'm a pretty good . . ." funnel" for what's happening in American theatre. I think we are in a public conversation—theatre you put out there is a public conversation with the audience. Playwrights should be aware of that, too. All the theatres in this city are in a public conversation and we're all mindful of what it is we're talking about and where is our place in the conversation. What are we adding to the conversation? I like to think I'm aware of that.

G: Should playwrights check with the theatre first before submitting a play? Maybe a general letter so they know what the theatre is looking for and what they're not looking for?

SG: Could save a lot of time.

G: In other words, I've written a mystery. You guys tend to shy away from them. If I check first I'll be saving you time and me postage.

SG: It never hurts a playwright to do some homework. Check out what you can about the theatre and the kind of stuff they tend to do.

G: It's been my experience with a new play that everyone has notes—and that's the way it should be. I want to know what the costumer thinks. The lighting designer, the sound designer . . ., etc. It's a collaborative art, after all. Have you met much resistance from playwrights when you offer suggestions?

SG: Sometimes. Playwrights have to remember that our mission is to put out the best version of the play we can and that requires an open mind. At the end of the day, however, it is still your play. A producer needs to be prepared to accept the version of the script they agreed to and stand by it. One should never assume that the changes you would like to see get made. You can't start rehearsals and "hope for the best." In the final analysis the play belongs to the writer, not the producer.

MARY HARDEN

Mary Harden has been an agent for over twenty-five years. She was a partner for many years in another firm. In 1996 she and her partner, Nancy Curtis, opened Harden-Curtis Associates, an agency that represents both actors and playwrights. The agency also represents their clients in film, television, and theatre. Her literary clients have plays produced on Broadway, off-Broadway, and regionally. Many of her clients also write for film and television.

Prior to becoming an agent Ms. Harden worked in the press and education departments of numerous regional theatres. She is a frequent guest panelist at the Dramatist Guild and the Academy of Television Art and Sciences, and is a member of the Board of Directors of the Dramatist Play Service. Bruce Graham interviewd her.

Graham: Every time I speak with aspiring playwrights the big question is, "How do I get an agent?"

Mary Harden: The question they should ask first is, "How do I get professional fans? How do I get people interested in me, my writing, and my career so that I have my own network?" I get a lot of my clients because artistic directors, dramaturgs, other playwrights, playwrights who teach recommend them to me. I will take query letters over the transom and read them. If I'm interested I'll ask to see the material, but usually it has to be somebody who has been produced or that I've heard about. The majority of the time the writers have had numerous productions before they get to me.

G: It's the old catch-22 thing sometimes. You can't get produced without an agent and you can't get an agent without getting produced. But at least with plays—as opposed to movie scripts—there are more outlets. At least for readings.

MH: Exactly. The theatre is a community.

G: Oh, that's good. I can use that.

MH: Well, it's true. Word of mouth among theatre professionals is very important. Often times I'll take on a playwright and I'm pretty sure I can't get that first play produced, but I know they're good writers. I know they're prolific. I'll send that first play out hoping people will recognize the quality of it and then—again hopefully—that second play is the one they want to produce. Because they've seen that first play—even though they didn't produce it—you as the playwright are a known quantity. And they tend to take you more seriously.

G: What's usually the problem with that "first" play?

MH: That's usually the autobiographical play that should have been kept in the drawer.

G: What you just said sounds like that scene from the movie *Prick Up Your Ears*. Where Vanessa Redgrave as the agent tells young playwright Joe Orton that his first play is "derivative"—but definitely wants to see the next one.

MH: Very true.

G: So basically, a lot of it is networking.

MH: Absolutely. That's why I tell people to go to schools where playwriting is taught by professional playwrights. They can answer questions about the business on top of teaching the skill. And hopefully they can steer you towards people.

G: Internships?

MH: One of the best things to do is an internship in a literary office somewhere. At least then you find out what people are looking for "on the other side."

G: Read scripts.

MH: Yes, read plays. You will also find out, for your own mental health, that people don't make decisions about your play based totally on merit. Sometimes it has to do with planning a season. Did they do a similar play last season? Then they might not want to do yours. Budget's a consideration. And interestingly enough, in most regional theatres that only do one new play a year, they are rarely going to pick a comedy.

G: Really? Why?

MH: Because they look for "serious" when they do new plays. It's a prestige thing. If they do two or three, they'll take a chance on a comedy.

G: One of the things I'm always telling my students is to do the intern thing. Get a foot in the door. Everyone is looking for someone to read scripts. It can be painful, but at the end of the day you can feel good about yourself when you realize, "Wow . . . there's a lot of real garbage out there." And lots of times you can learn more from a bad script than a good one. 'Cause if it's really good you're usually jealous.

Do specific agents look for plays written in a specific genre? In other words, are certain agents better for comedies than others while some are experts at dramas?

MH: Sometimes, with agents who have been around a while, you can get a feeling for what they like by seeing the writers they represent. But that doesn't hold to be one hundred percent true. You never know when an agent will respond to something new.

G: What do you look for?

MH: Plot. I like plot.

G: A lost art.

MH: I remember reading, very early on, Sam Shepard's *Buried Child*. When I saw it on the stage I thought it was brilliant. When I read it, however, I had no idea what it would have been on the stage. I am not the right agent for that play. An agent has to relate to the material and I wouldn't have known what to do with *Buried Child*. So you sort of have to recognize your own taste, but at the same time keep an open mind. Just because you don't respond doesn't mean it's a bad play.

G: So let's say the author now has a little bit of a track record. How do they go about actually finding the agent?

MH: Some belong to the Society of Author's Representatives, which may have a list of agents open to new work. If you think you write in the similar vein of a known playwright, try to find out who represents them. It's no guarantee but it gives you some sense of who's out there. There's some books out about agents, but it's mostly for movie scripts. Joining the Dramatist's Guild could also be a resource.

G: What the worst thing a playwright can do professionally?

MH: You mean besides leave nasty, threatening messages on a producer's answering machines?

G: Hey, that guy owed me money. I haven't done that in years.

MH: And we're all very proud. The worst thing . . . hmmmm . . . (A *long pause*) The worst thing is to believe the agent has the ability to get your play produced. It is very difficult not to have anger at the system. Not to feel rejected. Remember, the agent is on your side.

G: Let's talk about the procedure. I hand you the play. Then you do . . . what?

MH: I read it.

G: Good start.

MH: Unless I think it's not ready, I send it out. But things have changed in the last fifteen, twenty years. I really don't think you get a chance with a second draft these days. Very, very rarely. So I am more cautious now going out with a play than I was fifteen years ago. If I don't think it's ready to go out, I'll say something. But remember, I'm not the producer. If I have a problem with Scene Two in the second act I'm not going to say anything. The longer you have a relationship with a playwright, the more you come to know whether or not he's open to fixing things. I have to assume the playwright knows how to write. They don't need me telling them how to do that.

Also, I try not to prejudge. I try to send it to as wide a range of people as I can. You don't know what people will respond to. You think you know, but it's not always the case.

However, there are some theatres dedicated to doing nothing but new plays . . . and I've never had a client produced there. To me, that says our tastes are just not simpatico.

G: The regional theatre seems to have replaced New York as the developer of new plays.

MH: To a certain extent. It moves both ways. Like I said before, you're more likely to get a comedy done in New York City which will then go out and play the regionals, but a lot of those regionals wouldn't start it because it wasn't "arty" enough for them. The reality is that there is no more Broadway for straight plays.

The majority of New York theatre that will develop new plays is not-for-profit. When nonprofit theatres started years ago, that's when the regionals began to develop new plays. The mission became to discover and nurture new playwrights. Regional theatres have genuinely becomes a viable market-place. You don't have to have your play done in New York City to have a successful play. A play that has a life all over the country.

G: *Moon Over The Brewery* has never even come near New York, but it's my most produced play. Four characters. One set. And it's clean.

MH: There you have it.

G: It's the "clean" part that probably killed any chance in New York. Maybe I should've put in male nudity.

So, finally…a list of "do's" and "don'ts" for playwrights?

MH: Type legibly. Put it in the right form or I'm not going to look at it. I once represented a writer who didn't believe in killing trees and therefore single-spaced his entire play. I told him I can't get this done and I never will. Nobody will read it. Send a brief cover letter. Send a resume, or at least an explanation of who you are—what you've done, where you've gone to school. Keep it short. Have a title page and character page. You also have to be realistic: do not send out a three-hundred-page play.

Pet peeves: never write a play where the characters are called Faith, Hope, and Charity. And allegory. Never tell people it's an allegory.

G: I don't think people should call their plays "a comedy." What if nobody laughs? Let the audience decide.

MH: Right. Call it "a play."

If you expect to get material back always include the self addressed stamped envelope. Do not e-mail a script unless told to do so because nobody's going to pay to print out your script if they don't know what it is.

G: Well, that kills all my questions. Any parting advice for the aspiring play-wright?

MH (*Another long pause*): Make sure you have something to say.

PARTING WORDS

As you may have realized from the earlier chapters, Michele and I are pretty much in sync with the qualities we think are needed to write a good play. This is helpful professionally when we work together as dramaturg and playwright since it spares a lot of bloodshed and 911 calls.

We are also in agreement as teachers of playwriting; we both believe in the realities of the business. In other words, we try to scare the hell out of our students.

We've both observed classes taught by idealists with heavily rose-tinted glasses who speak glowingly of the beauty of art. They paint a glorious picture, but send students out unprepared for the realities of the professional theatre.

The truth is it's a very tough racket. If you don't believe us, pick up the Sunday New York Times and count how many plays are running off-Broadway. (And we stress off-Broadway because getting a straight play onto Broadway is next to impossible.)

The economics of New York theatre make it a very risky proposition to put a new, unproven play—even one that has successfully run in regional theatres—on the boards. My play According to Goldman has three characters and one set. Its budget is 800 grand. That's a sizeable chunk of cash.

So, to be quite honest, the odds of making a living as a playwright are pretty stiff. Even those of us who are supposedly "established" resort to movies, television, and teaching to supplement the royalty checks. (I've often said that the only writers who make less money than playwrights are poets. I've never heard of anyone living off the residuals from their hit poem.)

If you want to do this professionally you have to be open to any sort of reading or production when starting out. *Early One Evening at the Rainbow Bar & Grille* started out as a community theatre production. Eleven years later it made it to off-Broadway. So if your local college or community theatre says they'll take a shot with your new play, don't be a snob. Take 'em up on it. Trust us, you'll learn from it.

So why write for the theatre?

There's an intimate relationship with the audience you just can't get from film. If you are going to be a playwright, you cannot ever forget that it is for the audience that you are writing. A living, breathing, opinionated audience. They are not stupid, despite what many others might suppose. They will also help you take your play to the next level, making it better, richer, funnier and ultimately more enjoyable for you. They can also make your life a living hell, but you cannot forget about them.

The truth of the matter is you're probably not going to make that ton of money writing plays. You're not going on any talk shows or have your picture on the cover of *People* magazine. Ask most Americans to name three playwrights and chances are they'll come up with two: Shakespeare and Neil Simon.

Your real satisfaction should come from the audience. If that's what you're after, nothing Michele or I could ever say will frighten you away from writing for the theatre.